CUSTOM CURRICUL

Is Anybody There?

Fran and Jill Sciacca

Marion Duckworth

David C. Cook Publishing Co.
Elgin, Illinois—Weston, Ontario

Custom Curriculum
Is Anybody There?

Published by David C. Cook Publishing Co.
850 North Grove Ave., Elgin, IL 60120
Cable address: DCCOOK
Series creator: John Duckworth
Series editor: Randy Southern
Editor: Sharon Stultz
Option writers: Stan Campbell, Nelson E. Copeland, Jr., and Ellen Larson
Designer: Bill Paetzold
Cover illustrator: Michael Fleishman
Inside illustrator: Al Hering
Printed in U.S.A.

ISBN: 0-7814-5009-8

CONTENTS

About the Authors

Marion Duckworth is the author of several books, including *Why Teens Are Killing Themselves and What You Can Do about It* (Here's Life Publishers). She has spoken to church groups on subjects like self-image, and has taught young people in Sunday school. A former pastor's wife, she has worked with youth groups—and raised three teenagers.

Stan Campbell has been a youth worker for over eighteen years, and has written several books on youth ministry including the *BibleLog* series (SonPower) and the *Quick Studies* series (David C. Cook). He and his wife, Pam, are youth directors at Lisle Bible Church in Lisle, Illinois.

Nelson E. Copeland, Jr. is a nationally known speaker and the author of several youth resources including *Great Games for City Kids* (Youth Specialties) and *A New Agenda for Urban Youth* (Winston-Derek). He is president of the Christian Education Coalition for African-American Leadership (CECAAL), an organization dedicated to reinforcing educational and cultural excellence among urban teenagers. He also serves as youth pastor at the First Baptist Church in Morton, Pennsylvania.

Ellen Larson is an educator and writer with degrees in education and theology. She has served as minister of Christian education in several churches, teaching teens and children, as well as their teachers. Her experience also includes teaching in public schools. She is the author of several books for Christian education teachers, and frequently leads training seminars for volunteer teachers. Ellen and her husband live in San Diego and are the parents of two daughters.

You've Made the Right Choice!

Thanks for choosing **Custom Curriculum**! We think your choice says at least three things about you:

(1) You know your group pretty well, and want your program to fit that group like a glove;

(2) You like having options instead of being boxed in by some far-off curriculum editor;

(3) You have a small mole on your left forearm, exactly two inches above the elbow.

OK, so we were wrong about the mole. But if you like having choices that help you tailor meetings to fit your kids, **Custom Curriculum** *is* the best place to be.

Going through Customs

In this (and every) **Custom Curriculum** volume, you'll find

• five great sessions you can use anytime, in any order.

• reproducible student handouts, at least one per session.

• a truckload of options for adapting the sessions to your group (more about that in a minute).

• a helpful get-you-ready article by a youth expert.

• clip art for making posters, fliers, and other kinds of publicity to get kids to your meetings.

Each **Custom Curriculum** session has three to six steps. No matter how many steps a session has, it's designed to achieve these goals:

• *Getting together.* Using an icebreaker activity, you'll help kids be glad they came to the meeting.

• *Getting thirsty.* Why should kids care about your topic? Why should they care what the Bible has to say about it? You'll want to take a few minutes to earn their interest before you start pouring the "living water."

• *Getting the Word.* By exploring and discussing carefully selected passages, you'll find out what God has to say.

• *Getting the point.* Here's where you'll help kids make the leap from principles to nitty-gritty situations they are likely to face.

• *Getting personal.* What should each group member do as a result of this session? You'll help each person find a specific "next-step" response that works for him or her.

Each session is written to last 45 to 60 minutes. But what if you have less time—or more? No problem! **Custom Curriculum** is all about ... options!

What Are My Options?

Every **Custom Curriculum** session gives you fourteen kinds of options:

• *Extra Action*—for groups that learn better when they're physically moving (instead of just reading, writing, and discussing).

• *Combined Junior High/High School*—to use when you're mixing age levels, and an activity or case study would be too "young" or "old" for part of the group.

• *Small Group*—for adapting activities that would be tough with groups of fewer than eight kids.

• *Large Group*—to alter steps for groups of more than twenty kids.

• *Urban*—for fitting sessions to urban facilities and multiethnic (especially African-American) concerns.

• *Heard It All Before*—for fresh approaches that get past the defenses of kids who are jaded by years in church.

• *Little Bible Background*—to use when most of your kids are strangers to the Bible, or haven't made a Christian commitment.

• *Mostly Guys*—to focus on guys' interests and to substitute activities they might be more enthused about.

• *Mostly Girls*—to address girls' concerns and to substitute activities they might prefer.

• *Extra Fun*—for longer, more "rowdy" youth meetings where the emphasis is on fun.

• *Short Meeting Time*—tips for condensing the session to 30 minutes or so.

• *Fellowship & Worship*—for building deeper relationships or enabling kids to praise God together.

• *Media*—to spice up meetings with video, music, or other popular media.

• *Sixth Grade*—appearing only in junior high/middle school volumes, this option helps you change steps that sixth graders might find hard to understand or relate to.

• *Extra Challenge*—appearing only in high school volumes, this option lets you crank up the voltage for kids who are ready for more Scripture or more demanding personal application.

Each kind of option is offered twice in each session. So in this book, you get *almost 150* ways to tweak the meetings to fit your group!

Customizing a Session

All right, you may be thinking. *With all of these options flying around, how do I put a session together? I don't have a lot of time, you know.*

We know! That's why we've made **Custom Curriculum** as easy to follow as possible. Let's take a look at how you might prepare an actual meeting. You can do that in four easy steps:

(1) *Read the basic session plan.* Start by choosing one or more of the goals listed at the beginning of the session. You have three to pick from: a goal that emphasizes *knowledge*, one that stresses *understanding*, and one that emphasizes *action*. Choose one or more, depending on what *you* want to accomplish. Then read the basic plan to see what will work for you and what might not.

(2) *Choose your options.* You don't *have* to use any options at all; the

basic session plan would work well for many groups, and you may want to stick with it if you have absolutely no time to consider options. But if you want a more perfect fit, check out your choices.

As you read the basic session plan, you'll see small symbols in the margin. Each symbol stands for a different kind of option. When you see a symbol, it means that kind of option is offered for that step. Turn to the page noted by the symbol and you'll see that option explained.

Let's say you have a small group, mostly guys who get bored if they don't keep moving. You'll want to keep an eye out for three kinds of options: Small Group, Mostly Guys, and Extra Action. As you read the basic session, you might spot symbols that tell you there are Small Group options for Step 1 and Step 3—maybe a different way to play a game so that you don't need big teams, and a way to cover several Bible passages when just a few kids are looking them up. Then you see symbols telling you that there are Mostly Guys options for Step 2 and Step 4—perhaps a substitute activity that doesn't require too much self-disclosure, and a case study guys will relate to. Finally you see symbols indicating Extra Action options for Step 2 and Step 3—maybe an active way to get kids' opinions instead of handing out a survey, and a way to act out some verses instead of just looking them up.

After reading the options, you might decide to use four of them. You base your choices on your personal tastes and the traits of your group that you think are most important right now. **Custom Curriculum** offers you more options than you'll need, so you can pick your current favorites and plug others into future meetings if you like.

(3) *Use the checklist.* Once you've picked your options, keep track of them with the simple checklist that appears at the end of each option section (just before the start of the next session plan). This little form gives you a place to write down the materials you'll need too—since they depend on the options you've chosen.

(4) *Get your stuff together.* Gather your materials; photocopy any Repro Resources (reproducible student sheets) you've decided to use. And . . . you're ready!

The Custom Curriculum Challenge

Your kids are fortunate to have you as their leader. You see them not as a bunch of generic teenagers, but as real, live, unique kids. You care whether you really connect with them. That's why you're willing to take a few extra minutes to tailor your meetings to fit.

It's a challenge to work with real, live kids, isn't it? We think you deserve a standing ovation for taking that challenge. And we pray that **Custom Curriculum** helps you shape sessions that shape lives for Jesus Christ and His kingdom.

—The Editors

Relationship Deficiency Syndrome

by Fran and Jill Sciacca

Most teens are emotionally driven and motivated by personal experience rather than advice or education. Their feelings steer their lives. And their lives tend to migrate toward that which they feel, hear, taste, touch, and see. That translates into an obvious preference for the real world of people and events over that of the supernatural world that they cannot grasp.

So the idea of cultivating a relationship with someone (God) they cannot see, hear, or touch is foreign, impractical, and often undesirable. It involves too much effort, they believe, with too few immediate, tangible dividends.

Meaningful relationships are not an abundant commodity as we close this century, particularly from the viewpoint of most young people. Many have been disillusioned by divorced parents, fractured families, fickle friends, or authority figures who have morally or ethically disappointed them. To invest in a deep relationship may seem like a sure way to get hurt, let down, or both.

As you prepare to lead these sessions in *Is Anybody There?* realize that you are working with a generation that has been shortchanged. These young people lack role models, methods, and meaning in human relationships. Though most adults agree that our young people have been pampered more than any previous generation, we fail to see that their lack of interpersonal skills is a result of broken significant relationships in their lives. On the other hand, it is also true that young people *yearn* for depth in relationships. They *fear* it, yet they *seek* it.

Failure in the realm of human relationships makes success in the world of spiritual relationships difficult to understand. This is somewhat true for all of us. Sometimes we expect God to treat us as harshly as some hurtful, significant person in our lives has done. Thus, the potential for impact as you work through *Is Anybody There?* is profound!

You have the unique opportunity to introduce teens to an abiding friend who will never fail them. You stand in a place of privilege. The Lord can use you to be His vehicle to virtually transform the way a young person sees God and learns to relate to Him. Present a relationship unlike any other he or she has ever known or believed possible—one that is permanent, dependable, deeply personal, and meaningful.

The following are some helpful "big picture" insights. They are designed to color and clarify your perception as you study the concepts of *Is Anybody There?* They will prepare you to see this curriculum from the viewpoint of the learner as well as the leader.

Half of an Orange Is *Not* an Orange!

One morning I moved into my classroom of high-school juniors carrying half of an orange. As the pre-bell chatter began to dwindle, I held up the fruit and asked, "What do I have in my hand?"

"An orange!" said one indignant student.

"Nice try," I responded, "but not correct."

A wave of whispers rolled over the room as these astute young people tried to determine if I was merely massaging their minds or if they had really missed it.

"This is *not* an orange. It's half of an orange," I said. After some arguing, they agreed that I was right. What half of an orange is is determined by what a *whole* orange is. By now, you're probably perplexed, wondering what this has to do with cultivating a relationship with God. It has *a lot* to do with it!

Most young people in your group are probably "half orange" people. When it comes to what is real, they believe that the material world is real and the supernatural world is either less real or real in a different sense. Subconsciously they assume that the world inhabited by God, angels, and the spirits of departed people is not as real or as understandable as the world in which they live. As you work through the sessions in *Is Anybody There?* try to help your group members gain a fresh understanding of the following key concepts.

- The immaterial, spiritual world is as real as the material world.
- Being comfortable in the material world makes it seem more real to me. But my goal must be to learn how to become more at home in the spiritual world.
- As a Christian, I live in both worlds simultaneously. I do not have to go through some sort of entry procedure to connect with the world where God dwells. Both are related. What I do in one is not distinct from what happens in the other. Prayer, evangelism—all Christian living is carried out in both at the same time.
- If reality consists of both worlds, then we as Christians are the only people living in the "real world"! This is a tough concept, but a crucial one, because many teens consider the real world as the one enjoyed by nonbelievers. They feel stuck in a second-class world full of rules. Help them see that the real world is *not* the one where there are no boundaries or consequences. The *nonbeliever* actually abides in the fantasy world because he or she denies the existence of the supernatural.

Your goal is to get your group members to feel more aware of and at home in the spiritual world they are already in. God is with them at home, at school, in the lunchroom, on the sports field—even in the restroom!

Young people want to compartmentalize their lives into their "Christian life" (the way they act at church) and their "other life" (the way they act away from church). But these two worlds must be brought together in their minds because they *are* together. God is with your young people constantly. He watches them, wants to speak to them, help them, and have them obey Him.

As a high school Bible teacher, I tackle this compartmentalizing dilemma daily. Recently a student addressed a high school assembly about his summer missions trip to the former Soviet Union. Over there (in his "Christian life"), sacrifices for young believers were made easily. Several weeks into school this fall, however, this same student (in his "other life") made an underclassman and younger believer give up his bed and sleep on the floor at a weekend retreat so that *he* could have the whole bed! He apparently felt no tension and failed to see that his relationship with God in Kiev, which prompted his sacrifices for new Christians, should also be the driving force in *all* of his relationships *all* of the time.

In His Image, Start to Finish

A precious biblical truth in regard to cultivating a relationship with God is that we are made "in His . . . image" (Genesis 1:27). God does not have a physical body (John 4:24), so this image must have to do with that unseen part of us that really determines who we are as individuals. Simply put, God and I have something in common. I am not God, or even *a* god. But, I am "like God" in terms of who I am.

Therefore, my ability to feel, think, communicate, decide, choose, and a host of other human activities are actually abilities I share with God Himself. Young people need to know that God made us this way so that we could have a moment-by-moment relationship with Him. We can talk to Him, tell Him our feelings and fears. He understands our darkest thoughts—not because He feels the same way we do, but because He does feel, think, and choose.

Jesus Christ, God in a body, demonstrates this truth in Technicolor. We see in Christ all that humanity ought to be. Jesus took upon Himself our humanity to redeem us. But He did not sacrifice His deity in the process.

Cultivating a personal relationship with the God in whose image we were created not only makes sense, it is also the deepest cry of a person's soul, both for the young and the old. People were *made* for this relationship. We know that something is amiss without it. As you work through *Is Anybody There?* hold before your group a relationship that is attainable, permanent, and fulfilling. In fact, you can do so with confidence, knowing that it is the very thing for which you were created.

Communicate that "walking with God" is an awesome adventure in the real world. It is not simply a code of conduct that you live at church and then leave there. God loves us and deeply desires a moment-by-moment relationship with us. He wants to enter every area of our lives and reveal Himself to us. He awaits our call. To the lonely, sometimes perplexing question "Is anybody there?" we answer "Yes! Always!"

Fran and Jill Sciacca have been involved with youth ministry for nearly two decades. Fran has been teaching high school Bible since 1980 in a large Christian school serving students from over 180 local churches. Jill has a degree in journalism and sociology and is a full-time homemaker and free-lance writer/editor. She has written for Discipleship Journal *and* Decision *magazine, and has served on the editorial team for the* Youth Bible *(Word). Fran and Jill coauthored* Lifelines *(Zondervan), an award-winning Bible study series for high schoolers. Fran is the author of the best-selling Bible study,* To Walk and Not Grow Weary *(NavPress), as well as* Generation at Risk *(Moody), and* Wounded Saints *(Baker).*

Publicity Clip Art

The images on these two pages are designed to help you promote this course within your church and community. Feel free to photocopy anything here and adapt it to fit your publicity needs. The stuff on this page could be used as a flier that you send or hand out to kids—or as a bulletin insert. The stuff on the next page could be used to add visual interest to newsletters, calendars, bulletin boards, or other promotions. Be creative and have fun!

Is Anybody There?

How can we know if God is really there? How close does God want us to be to Him? If God speaks, why do we have so much trouble hearing Him? How does the Holy Spirit "live" in us? What does it really mean to "walk" with God? We'll be looking at questions like these as we begin a new course called *Is Anybody There?* Come and learn how to strengthen your most important relationship.

Who:

When:

Where:

Questions? Call:

Is Anybody There?

Is Anybody There?

Is anybody there?

Can we prove that God exists?

Does God really speak to us?

(Write your own message in the speech balloon.)

SESSION

1

How Do I Know He's Really There?

YOUR GOALS FOR THIS SESSION:

Choose one or more

☐ To help kids recognize that it makes sense to believe in God.

☐ To help kids understand that God is interested in them.

☐ To give kids an opportunity to establish or renew their relationship with God as Father.

☐ Other ______________________________
____

Your Bible Base:

Isaiah 55:6, 7
Acts 17:24-28
Galatians 3:26–4:7
Ephesians 1:4, 5

What Is Real?

(Needed: Cut-apart copy of Repro Resource 1)

Have group members form two teams. Instruct the teams to face each other. Distribute half of the descriptions from "Astonishing Animals" (Repro Resource 1) to Team A and half to Team B. Explain that some of the descriptions are real and some are fake. Team A is to read aloud a description as convincingly as possible and Team B is to guess whether the animal is real or fake, based on the description. Then Team B will read a description and Team A will guess. Continue until the teams run out of descriptions. The team with the most correct guesses at the end of the game wins.

Afterward, ask: **How hard was it to decide whether the animals were real or not? If it was difficult, what made it difficult?** (Some group members might say it was difficult because *all* of the animals sounded pretty weird and amazing.)

How might these animals point to the existence of a Creator? (They're so unusual, unique, and creatively formed that it seems logical to believe that only a divine Creator could have made them.)

What are some other things that seem to point to the existence of a Creator? (The human body, the stars and the universe, trees and plant life, etc.) If no one mentions it, suggest that the Bible is a piece of evidence testifying to God's existence.

Let's say that God really does exist. So what? Why should it matter to us? Get as many responses as possible.

STEP 2

Who Is God, Anyway?

(Needed: Chalkboard and chalk or newsprint and marker, index cards, pencils, paper)

Write the following unfinished sentences on the board.

• "Sometimes I feel as though God is . . ."

• "I wish that God . . ."

Distribute index cards and pencils. Have group members complete the sentences and return the cards to you. They should not write their names on the cards. After you've collected the cards, shuffle them and read them aloud. Use the following suggestions to supplement group members' responses.

• Sometimes I feel as though God is "mad at me"; "not interested in me"; "far away"; "frightening"; etc.

• I wish that God "was visible"; "talked to me"; "was easier to get to know"; etc.

Explain: **People often feel that God is far away, that He doesn't care about them, or that He is too important to be interested in them. If you feel that way, you're normal. But you also need to take a look at facts about God. Let's see what Scripture says about God's relationship with us.**

Write the following questions and Scripture references on the board:

1. Why should I think about God anyway? (Acts 17:24-28)

2. Where is God and how does He want me to act toward Him? (Isaiah 55:6, 7)

3. What kind of relationship does God want to have with me and how does it begin? (Galatians 3:26–4:7)

Have group members form three teams. Assign each team one of the questions on the board. Instruct each team to look up its assigned passage and answer the question, using personal pronouns like "I" and "me" in their responses. Distribute paper and pencils to each team so team members can record their answers.

Give the teams several minutes to work. When they're finished, have each team share its response. Use the following suggestions to supplement the teams' answers.

(1) I should think about God because He is my Creator and decides when and where people should live. He wants me to think about Him and reach out to Him. He is the source of my life.

(2) He is not far from me and wants me to reach out to Him, seek

Him, pray, turn from sin, and turn to Him for forgiveness.

(3) God wants to be my Father and wants me to be His son or daughter. He wants to make me an heir of all He owns. I can become His son or daughter when I place my personal faith in Jesus Christ as Savior.

Say: **If you were drowning in a lake or hanging from a cliff and a hand reached out to save you, you would really want to have a relationship with that hand. A relationship with that hand—and its owner—would be of prime importance to you at that moment. So why do you think God wants to have a relationship with people, even though we're not critical to His survival?**

If your group members have trouble coming up with answers, give them the following Scripture passages to look up. Or even if they have some ideas, they may not be able to come up with evidence from Scripture. In that case, you can write their ideas on the board, give them the references to look up, and have them match their statements with the appropriate references.

Here are some reasons why God wants to have a relationship with us:

- We were chosen according to His will (Ephesians 1:11).
- It gives Him pleasure (Ephesians 1:5).
- The result of not having a relationship with Him now is separation from Him forever. God does not want anyone to suffer that fate (II Peter 3:9).
- He loves us (Ephesians 2:4-7).

A Special Relationship

Have your group members sit in a circle on the floor for a brainstorming game. The object of the game is to list as many "famous pairs" as possible. Each person will have five seconds to name a famous pair. If he or she cannot name one or names a pair that has already been used, he or she is out. Continue the game until only one person remains.

Write group members' responses on the board as they are named. Use the following suggestions to supplement their ideas.

- Bert and Ernie (from *Sesame Street*)
- Peanut butter and jelly

- Batman and Robin
- Road Runner and Wile E. Coyote
- Abbott and Costello
- Burgers and fries
- Chip and Dale
- DeGarmo and Key (Christian recording artists)
- Mickey Mouse and Minnie Mouse
- Wayne and Garth (from *Wayne's World*)
- David and Goliath

Briefly discuss the relationship that the members of each pair have with each other. For example, you could point out that the Road Runner and Wile E. Coyote have an antagonistic relationship, to say the least, because one is always trying to eat the other.

After you've had some fun with this activity, get group members thinking about their relationships with God by adding "God and I" to the list on the board. Have group members think about which pair relationship listed on the board is most similar to their relationship with God. For example, some group members may think that their relationship with God is antagonistic, like the relationship between David and Goliath. Others may think their relationship with God is more like that of Bert and Ernie—a friendship. Invite volunteers to explain their ideas, but don't pressure anyone.

Afterward, say: **God wants to have a relationship with all of us. But His relationship with each one of us is unique because we are so different from one another. Nobody else has your DNA. Nobody else has your fingerprints. Nobody else has your exact personality. So nobody else can have the exact relationship with God that you can have.**

Let's take a look at how different we are. Then we'll be able to better understand why our relationships with God are unique.

Label one side of the room "A" and the other side "B." Explain that you will be reading several pairs of opposite personality characteristics ("A" and "B"). After you read each pair, group members will move to the "A" side of the room if Characteristic A best describes them. They will move to the "B" side of the room if Characteristic B best describes them. Group members will move from one side of the room to the other as often as necessary as you go through the list. If some kids say that neither statement applies, tell them to choose the one that they identify with most or stand somewhere between the two points.

(1) Characteristic A—I can yak it up with the best of them.
Characteristic B—I'm pretty quiet.

(2) Characteristic A—I like to read.
Characteristic B—If it weren't for the TV listings, I probably wouldn't read at all.

(3) Characteristic A—I laugh easily.
Characteristic B—I don't laugh very often.

OPTIONS

(4) Characteristic A—I flip through TV channels a lot.
Characteristic B—I can't stand it when people flip through TV channels.
(5) Characteristic A—I'm pretty trusting of other people.
Characteristic B—I'm pretty suspicious of other people.
(6) Characteristic A—I am neat and tidy.
Characteristic B—I usually just drop my things wherever I happen to be.
(7) Characteristic A—I enjoy watching sports on TV.
Characteristic B—I think watching sports on TV is a boring waste of time.
(8) Characteristic A—I'm patient enough to untie a tangled knot in my shoelace.
Characteristic B—I usually let knots stay knotted.
(9) Characteristic A—I'm pretty good about controlling my temper.
Characteristic B—I have a low boiling point and can "explode" easily.
(10) Characteristic A—I'm most alert late at night.
Characteristic B—I'm most alert early in the morning.

Afterward, say: **Most likely, no one else moved in the same pattern that you did from wall to wall. And even if someone did move the same as you, he or she still didn't have the same feelings about each statement as you did. For instance, concerning the first two statements, you may talk a lot more than a friend, yet you may have both leaned against the "yak it up" wall. The point is that we are all very different. So God deals with us differently.**

Coming Close

(Needed: Copies of Repro Resource 2)

Say: **Even though none of us can remember being born, there is one thing about it that you can know for sure: Not only was it tough on your mom, it was also probably tough on you. You probably were squeezed and pushed and twisted every which way. No doubt about it, being born was not easy!**

By the same token, you may feel that being born into God's family isn't easy either. You may feel as if God is a faraway stranger, despite what the Bible says. Let's take a look at a true story that might shed some light on what it takes to begin a relationship with God.

Distribute copies of "Jillian's Journey" (Repro Resource 2). After group members have had time to read the sheet, ask: **What similarity do you see between the way Jillian's relationship with her parents began and the way our relationship with God begins?** (Both begin with adoption.) Have someone read aloud Ephesians 1:4, 5.

Then say: **Jillian was abused by foster parents so she was afraid to trust the Ryans. While God hasn't abused us, some kids might feel nervous about trusting Him. What might be some reasons?** (They might have some wrong ideas about God and don't know what He's really like. They might have had some bad things happen to them and blame God for it. People may have been mean to them, causing them to think that God acts the same way.)

What did Jillian's new parents do to change her mind? (They remained patient and kept showing their love for her.)

Point out that because God loves us, He waits for us to reach out to Him. If you think some of your group members need to accept Christ as Savior, read aloud John 1:12 and explain that they can receive Him into their lives today. Invite those who are interested to see you after the session is over.

Say: **Receiving Christ as Savior is only the beginning of your relationship. Once God is your Father, you'll spend the rest of your life getting to know Him better.**

As you wrap up the session, remind group members that the three principles in Acts 17:27 are always true. You may want to write them on the board:

1. God wants us to reach out to Him.
2. If we do, we will find Him.
3. He isn't far from each one of us.

Close the session in prayer, thanking God for choosing to reach out to us.

Astonishing Animals

1. The mute swan's nine-foot wingspan is so powerful that it can break a person's bones. (True)

2. Some bald eagles' nests weigh as much as several tons. (True)

3. Each year, the canary learns a new repertoire of songs to sing to attract female birds, never singing the old songs again. (True)

4. The male crab shakes hands with the female with whom he chooses to mate. (True)

5. Koko, a gorilla, was taught to use its voice to speak human language. Koko also had a puppy for a pet. (False. Koko learned sign language and had a kitten for a pet.)

6. When a female lobster sheds her shell, the male lobster eats it. (True)

7. The Japanese goldfish contains a poison so powerful that one drop can kill a human. (True)

---

8. The cicada, an insect, lays its eggs in twigs. The young hatch and burrow into the ground where they stay 4-20 years, before emerging. (True)

9.The "sloth" is rightly named because it's lazy and dull-witted. (False. The sloth, whose name means "lazy," was thought to be that kind of animal. Now we know that it was designed to use as little energy as possible so it can survive on a diet of leaves.)

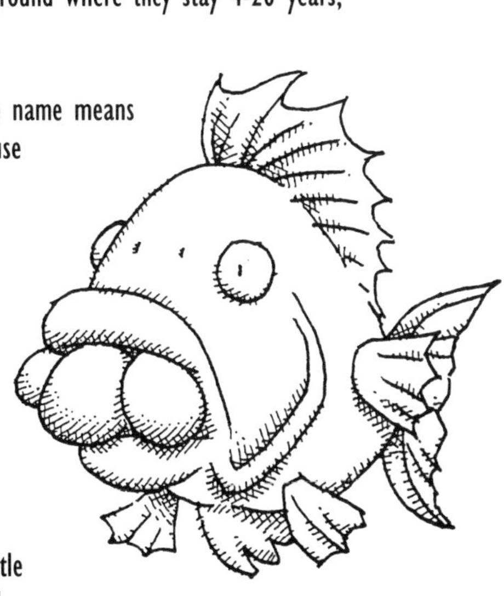

10. The tilapia macrocephala fish carries its fertilized eggs in its mouth and doesn't eat until the little ones are born. (True)

11. The guiana termite has a "squirt gun"-like appendage on its head, which it uses to "shoot" invaders. (True)

12. The mudskipper fish can climb trees. (True)

13. Cowbirds, appropriately named because they follow cattle and eat the grain the cattle leave, are among the best parents in the bird kingdom. (False. Cowbirds do follow cattle and eat grain, but they lay their eggs in the nests of other birds, hoping that the unsuspecting "foster parents" will raise their young.)

14. The necrophorus beetle is the "undertaker" of the insect world because it buries dead animals. (True)

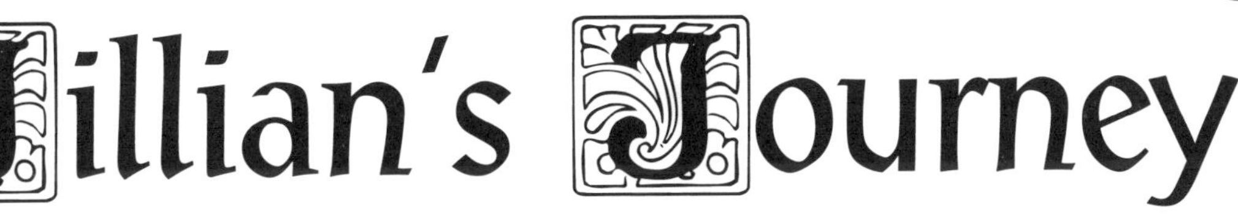

Jillian's Journey

Jillian was adopted when she was eight years old. The Ryans, her new parents, were excited to have her as their daughter. One way they showed their excitement was by preparing a beautiful bedroom for her. In it, there were lots of toys and a desk of her own—complete with crayons, pencils, and paper.

"But my years of misery couldn't be erased by an adoption ceremony," Jillian recalls. "Hurt and anger still boiled inside me.

"I found that it is one thing to need love...

to want it desperately...

to cry for it...

but quite another thing to *accept* love when it is offered."

That's because, before age eight, Jillian had been rejected, humiliated, neglected, and abused by a series of foster parents. Once she was locked out of the house overnight to stay in the dark with "monsters."

Because of her bad experiences, it took Jillian years to be able to feel close to her parents and to accept their love. Now, though, she is able to do that.

Today, Jillian is a successful Christian recording artist who travels around the world telling others to let God love them. (From *Please, Somebody, Love Me!* by Jillian and Joseph A. Ryan, Baker Book House, Grand Rapids, MI, 1991.)

OPTIONS

S E S S I O N O N E

Step 1
As soon as you finish the "Astonishing Animals" quiz on Repro Resource 1, ask: **What is something you can do that, if someone happened to see you do it, might qualify you for his or her list of astonishing animals?** Give group members a few minutes to think of an unusual talent or to find nearby props that might be needed. Make sure everyone knows that you're not expecting anything complicated. Most young people, however, have perfected particular sound effects, facial expressions, or goofy mannerisms—perhaps something handed down from parents. If time permits, let each person demonstrate his or her talent individually. If not, give a signal for everyone to *simultaneously* begin. (Try to position group members so that they can see everyone else while performing their own talents.)

Step 3
Rather than have group members brainstorm the famous pairs, write the pairs down ahead of time on individual slips of paper (adding others of your own) and let group members play charades. Before you begin, pair up students and let them know in what order they are to participate. Each pair of students should quickly draw a slip from the "Famous Pairs" stack and assume the roles of the pair listed there. As soon as someone else guesses the famous pair, those two students should rejoin the group as the next two students *immediately* draw another slip from the pile. Try to maintain an intensity to the pace of this activity. Charades can drag if you allow it to, but it can generate a lot of activity if you keep the action going and make sure everyone stays involved.

Step 1
Small groups often feel they cannot do things large groups do, so try to capitalize on opportunities you have that large groups *don't*. Since one of the themes running throughout this session is being aware that God is definitely nearer than we sometimes realize, consider going "on the road" to look for indications of His presence. If possible, borrow a van and hold your meeting as you drive along some back roads, parks, or other scenic areas. Your discussions and Bible study can be done as usual, but you will have the added opportunity to observe the wonders of creation as you drive around. Even the "A" and "B" sides of the room in Step 3 can be adapted to "Front" and "Back" of the van. (If you are the only adult, it is probably too much of a challenge to drive and teach at the same time, but you could still drive to a more remote spot, park, and then teach.)

Step 4
Even if you don't choose to hold the meeting in a moving vehicle (see the "Small Group" option for Step 1), consider ending it by retiring to a small and confining space (a closet, the pastor's office, or some other tight area). Discuss how we sometimes take for granted the amount of "space" we have. (In some countries, the sidewalks, trains, buses, and so forth are almost always overcrowded.) But sometimes we begin to feel *too* removed from other people. As you stay packed closely together, the discussion of the discomfort of being born will likely take on a new reality. And as you end the session by reminding everyone that God isn't far from each one of us, the closeness will be an object lesson. End with a challenge: **The next time you feel isolated and alone, try to remember this feeling. God is always just this close. If we are willing to reach out, we discover that He is already right there.**

Step 1
In a large group, don't use Repro Resource 1 as a handout. Rather, read one example at a time and let group members respond individually. To ensure complete honesty, have group members write down their answers. If your group is competitive, you could even make this an elimination game. Begin with everyone standing as you read the first description; then have each person record his or her answer. Those who answer correctly remain standing while the others sit down. Anyone standing at the end is certainly an unusual animal in his or her own right. And if everyone is sitting before the end of the list, start over again and give everyone another chance.

Step 3
Pair up your group members before you get ready to brainstorm famous couples. Then, rather than have them name the couples, have the members of each pair strike a pose (simultaneously) to represent a famous couple they have thought of. As they hold the pose, go around the room and let the members of each pair say who they are portraying. The first time through, you will probably get some of the basic, expected couples. But with a large group, you can do this several times and create a long list of famous pairs in a short amount of time. The more times you do this, the more creative your students will be in coming up with pairs of people or things.

OPTIONS

S E S S I O N   O N E

Step 2
If your group members are well acquainted with the basics of God's love and availability, you might want to cover the same material by having them roleplay a situation in which they are forced to share what they know—or think they know. Ask two volunteers to pretend that they are shipwrecked on an island where the natives have never heard about God. The natives, rather than being ignorant savages, should be very intelligent and sophisticated. The rest of the group members should play the natives, who observe the shipwrecked people thanking God for safety in reaching land and then begin to quiz the people about this "God" they were speaking to.

Step 4
It is common for young people to think they know all about God—until their knowledge is questioned. Given time to prepare, they may come up with the right answers. But an unanticipated question might catch them off guard. If possible, try to arrange a "plant" to sit through the session—someone your group members think is a first-time visitor, but who actually is a young, mature Christian from another church. The person should pretend to absorb what is discussed throughout the session. But as the meeting draws to a close, he or she should ask these questions:
• "How can you guys be so sure that God exists when you can't see Him?"
• "Do you really believe that just thinking about God brings Him closer?"
• "Even if God exists, do you expect me to believe that He cares about a regular person like me?"
• "Are you telling me that my life is going to change drastically if I just decide today that I'm going to believe in God and follow Christ? Just how does that work?"

When the questions begin, quickly toss them to the group to handle. When *you* ask the questions, your kids probably feel pretty sure about the answers. But see how well they do when the questions are being asked by a total stranger.

Step 2
Even though each portion of Scripture in this section is short, there are quite a few references for group members who don't know their way around the Bible very well. To make this step a bit less intimidating for such students, you might consider simply talking your way through the questions and answers, focusing on just one or two of the passages you feel are most important to your group members. Then, at the end of the session, provide lists of the Bible passages you used during the session. (Or provide a single list and let everyone copy down the passages.) Challenge students to use these verses/passages as texts for personal devotions during the week as they continue to think about the things you have discussed. (Appropriately, there are seven separate Bible references given in this section.) As inexperienced group members begin to explore the Bible on their own—at their own pace—they will become more comfortable with Bible study.

Step 3
If your group members don't know much about God, it may be difficult for them to think in terms of a close relationship with someone they cannot see, hear, or feel. You might want to deal with the concept of God by having kids try to think in terms of a perfect parent. Could they relate to a parent who loved them no matter what they did wrong? One who could discipline them without yelling or making them feel worthless? One who cared about their innermost hopes, dreams, and fears? Tie this concept into a challenge for increased Bible involvement. Say: **We aren't given instruction manuals to know how we need to relate to our parents. But we do have a wonderful manual to show us how we can have the best possible relationship with our perfect heavenly parent.** If group members see the personal benefit, rather than the obligation of Bible study, they may be willing to become more involved.

Step 1
Before you ask group members to list things that seem to point to the existence of a Creator, lay out a large piece of newsprint and have them create a "reminder mural." Rather than *naming* things, have group members *draw* them instead. It should be fairly simple to illustrate the stars and universe on one portion of the mural as well as the earthly reminders in another portion. Keep your mural in view as you go through this session (and any other sessions in this series) as a reminder of things to be thankful for. Your students can continue to add items to the mural as they continue their study of God's presence in their lives.

Step 4
After you read Jillian's story on Repro Resource 2, keep the discussion on a personal level rather than a spiritual one as you deal with the concept of adoption. Ask: **If you were being adopted, what do you think would be your main fears or concerns?** Record group members' answers. *Then* move on to the spiritual significance of adoption. It should quickly become clear that God would never be abusive to His adopted children. God would not play favorites by giving some people privileges that others don't have. God wouldn't lose interest in the ones He adopts. With all the negative publicity concerning adoption and foster homes, adoption may have bad connotations. Yet when God is the adopting parent, we have great cause for celebration. You might want to use a red marker to put a dot on each person's hand to remind him or her that even though we are adopted individually, we become "blood brothers" as we serve the same Father in Christian fellowship.

Step 2
Have your group members complete their sentences on index cards and return them to you. As you read each anonymous statement, ask group members to decide whether they think most people agree with that statement or disagree with it. (They do not need to indicate how they feel personally.) Have those who think most people would agree with it move to one side of the room, and those who think most people would disagree with it move to the other side of the room. While group members are still standing in position, ask volunteers on each side to explain why they responded as they did.

Step 4
After discussing "Jillian's Journey" (Repro Resource 2), ask your group members to think about their own response to God's love. Distribute paper and pencils. Instruct each person to write a personal journal entry in response to one of these statements: **"God doesn't really love me all that much," "I know God loves me enough to die for me, but I don't want His love,"** or **"I know God loves me enough to die for me and my response is . . ."** Have group members write for three to five minutes. Then ask for volunteers to share what they've written. Afterward, suggest that group members take their entries home and add to them as they learn more about the nature of God and His love.

Step 3
When you begin to describe each individual's relationship with God, try to incorporate the concept of God as a coach. Let guys who have been on sports teams describe the characteristics of a good coach: motivating the team to work together, helping individuals identify and strengthen weaknesses, expecting the best possible performance from everyone involved, providing instruction and assurance throughout the game, challenging everyone to maintain a daily regimen of personal development, and so forth. Be forewarned that some people may have had negative experiences with poor coaches; but some of the strongest bonds young people form with adults are with coaches who help them realize (to some degree) what their inner potential might be. Help your group members realize that God can provide the leadership and support of the best coach they can ever imagine.

Step 4
Rather than handing out copies of Repro Resource 2, simply read it and let your group members know that Jillian's story is true. But before you begin to discuss it, adapt the circumstances to a masculine point of view. Rather than a beautiful bedroom with toys, desk, crayons, pencils, and paper, let them envision a large yard with a tree house and baseball diamond. The feelings that are evoked are likely to be the same, but male group members will be more likely to relate to specifics from their own childhoods. Be sensitive to their feelings. We sometimes tend to assume that young boys are not as sensitive to emotions of fear, distrust, suspicion, etc. as young girls are. But at such an early age, there is little difference in the way people respond to such things. Teenage boys might be more reluctant than teenage girls to express how they feel now (or at age eight), but their feelings are just as strong.

Step 1
Before you hand out Repro Response 1, play "Barnyard." Divide into two teams of equal size. Put the teams at opposite ends of a large room. Assign everyone at one end of the room the name of a barnyard animal. Then assign the same animal names to the group members at the other end. Blindfold everyone (or have group members keep their eyes closed) and explain that the goal is to find the other animal of one's own species by making the noise of that animal. (Cows should moo, ducks should quack, etc.) With everyone making noise at the same time and unable to see, this isn't as easy as it sounds. Afterward, move right into the "Astonishing Animals" segment of the meeting.

Step 3
When you get to the section in which you are discussing each person's uniqueness through DNA, fingerprints, and so forth, let students create a more tangible reflection of their own individuality. Pull out a stamp pad and squares of paper and ask group members to create "thumbprint people." They should ink their thumbs, make a clear print on the paper, and then create a person from the print. The dress, expression, surrounding, and possessions of the thumbprint person should reflect the group member's own personality and interests. Football players might want to draw helmets and shoulder pads, and surround the figure with goal posts and cheerleaders. Musicians might want to draw the appropriate instrument for the thumbprint person to play. Any number of creative, individual, and unique applications can be made from each person's unique and individual thumbprint.

S E S S I O N   O N E

Step 3

After you brainstorm the famous pairs, help kids think about the "God and me" relationship by having them create a TV pilot for a new series called "God and Me." Have them consider these questions:

- **Who will be the main character?**
- **What is the setting of the show?**
- **Since a good show has good conflict, what will be the conflict of this series?**
- **What are some silly things the main character does to resolve the conflict?**
- **How would God be represented in this show? If visually, who would be the actor? If just a voice is used, whose voice would it be?**

Try not to let the discussion get too flippant where God is involved, but challenge kids to think creatively. If they truly believe that God is a major influence in their lives, they may need to consider new and better ways to relate to Him.

Step 4

As you invite people to consider beginning a relationship with God, have kids think in terms of joining a fan club. Ask:

- **If new Christians could join a "New Kids in the Flock Fan Club," what would be the requirements for membership?**
- **What would be the primary benefits of being members?**
- **What do people do to show support when they really like a rock star or other hero?** (Read material about him or her, listen closely to song lyrics, go to concerts, talk about the person with friends, etc.)
- **Why do you think we can get so excited about a sports hero or rock group, while at the same time we may find church stuff so "boring"?**
- **Do you think anyone deserves our support and enthusiasm more than God does?**
- **How do you think we can get more excited about our faith?**

Step 1

This step (and most of the others) can be abbreviated so you can teach the whole session without eliminating any entire activities. You can choose a couple of animals from Repro Resource 1 rather than dividing into teams and doing them all. In Step 2, rather than having kids write out their responses to the two unfinished sentences, ask for verbal responses. Also deal with the Bible portions as a single group rather than dividing into teams. In Step 3, the "A" or "B" choices can be determined by show of hands rather than moving around the room. By revising these few things, you can save a great deal of time overall.

Step 2

If you still feel you need to shave a few minutes, you as leader can summarize the content of this step as a mini-lecture. Otherwise, kids usually take quite a bit of time dividing into groups, looking up several verses, answering predetermined questions, and so forth. You can regulate their pace by "walking them through" what you want them to know and asking just enough questions to ensure that they're staying with you. That should also give them time to participate in most of the other activities and experiences.

Step 1

Here are some urban additions to "Astonishing Animals" (Repro Resource 1):

(1) Many city pigeons sleep in crevices on buildings. (Correct.)
(2) All alley cats live in alleys. (Wrong.)
(3) Some rats are as big as cats. (Correct.)
(4) A trained dog will never turn against its owner. (Wrong.)

Step 3

Another option for this activity is to name the first person of a famous pair and see if group members can name the other. You could make the activity competitive by having group members form two teams and awarding a point to the first team that responds correctly. You might want to use some of the following suggestions for an urban audience.

- **Ike Turner** (Tina Turner)
- **Kid** (Play)
- **Lone Ranger** (Tonto)
- **Salt** (Peppa)
- **Bullwinkle** (Rocky)

Point out that when we hear the name of one member of these pairs, we automatically think of the other.

Ask: **When people think of you, do they automatically think of someone else too?** (Some teens form friendship duos so tight that one person is never seen without the other.)

Say: **If you are really living the Christian life to the fullest, people will always see that you are in a relationship with God.**

Step 1
Junior highers are a lot more motivated when it comes to "doing" than they are with "thinking." Therefore, let them do Repro Resource 1 as written. But as you make the transition into discussing other things that seem to point to the existence of a Creator, make this a *doing* exercise. Have everyone go outside and find something to bring back and *show* as an evidence of God's creative skill. (Be sure to set a time limit.) Most junior highers won't mind turning over a few rocks, climbing trees, or getting a little dirty to come up with just the right artifact for their presentation. In addition, it allows them to get rid of a little restless energy at the beginning of the session.

Step 2
High schoolers should have no problem with the session as is, but junior highers might have a bit of difficulty finding the right words in this step to describe their thoughts and feelings about God. For many of them, it will be much easier (and more natural) to draw out their mental images of God. So rather than using the unfinished sentences, you might instruct them to draw God as they perceive Him. Or you might ask them to draw pictures to demonstrate the relationships they have with God. As with the unfinished sentences, you are likely to discover a variety of responses: fear, distance, protection, confusion, etc.

Step 2
The analogies of drowning or hanging from a cliff are only mentioned in passing, yet they offer a strong mental image. Divide your students into two teams. Ask each team to quickly create a skit—one with a drowning person and the other with a person dangling from the top of a cliff. Each skit should deal with the possible "hands" that reach out to the person and how the desperate person would respond to each one. (One hand might belong to a small child, unable to help. One might belong to a beautiful girl—someone half the size of the victim. One hand might belong to a very rich person who doesn't want to get his expensive clothes dirty. Or what if the victim is a white racist and the helping hand is black?) Through the skits, group members should see that the desire to be rescued is only one issue. Equally important is the ability of the other person to provide any real help.

Step 4
To emphasize the issue of adoption, ask your group members to consider sponsoring a child through a reliable organization that seeks aid for starving children. Most such organizations will provide pictures of the children, and the exchange of cards and letters. The monthly cost is not usually high; yet this is not something your group members should commit to unless they are absolutely certain that the money will continue for the prescribed time. If your kids are interested in becoming "adoptive parents," you might check with one or both of the following organizations:

Compassion International
P. O. Box 7000
Colorado Springs, CO 80933
1-800-336-7676

World Vision
Childcare Sponsorship
P. O. Box 1131
Pasadena, CA 91131
1-800-777-5777

Date Used:

Approx. Time

Step 1: What Is Real? ______
o Extra Action
o Small Group
o Large Group
o Fellowship & Worship
o Extra Fun
o Short Meeting Time
o Urban
o Combined Junior High/High School
Things needed:

Step 2: Who Is God, Anyway? ______
o Heard It All Before
o Little Bible Background
o Mostly Girls
o Short Meeting Time
o Combined Junior High/High School
o Extra Challenge
Things needed:

Step 3: A Special Relationship ______
o Extra Action
o Large Group
o Little Bible Background
o Mostly Guys
o Extra Fun
o Media
o Urban
Things needed:

Step 4: Coming Close ______
o Small Group
o Heard It All Before
o Fellowship & Worship
o Mostly Girls
o Mostly Guys
o Media
o Extra Challenge
Things needed:

SESSION 2

How Close Does God Want to Be to Me?

YOUR GOALS FOR THIS SESSION:

Choose one or more

☐ To help kids recognize the kind of closeness God wants to have with them.

☐ To help kids understand that their friendships with God can be real.

☐ To help kids develop an intimate relationship with God.

☐ Other ______________________________

Your Bible Base:

Genesis 1:26, 27; 2:18; 3:8, 9, 21
John 15:1-8
Romans 8:35-39
James 2:23

Too Close for Comfort

Have group members form pairs. Explain that the members of each pair should try to follow your instructions while they stand nose to nose. Read each of the following instructions one at a time, giving the pairs a chance to complete it before moving on to the next one.

- **Touch your toes.**
- **Walk in a circle.**
- **Sit down.**
- **Each of you take off one shoe.**
- **Shake hands with the members of another pair.**
- **Nod yes.**
- **Stand back to back.**
- **Pretend to wash your face.**
- **Hop on one foot.**

Afterward, ask: **Why did you have trouble following some of the instructions?** (Because we were "attached," we didn't have much freedom to move.)

Which instruction was impossible? (Standing back to back.)

What do you think it be like to be a Siamese twin joined at the nose? Get a few responses.

Say: **It's nice to be close to people, but not that close. But what about God? How close can we get to Him? How close do you want to get to Him?** Encourage most of your group members to offer their opinions.

Voices from the Past

(Needed: Bibles, chalk and chalkboard, copies of Repro Resource 3)

Ask: **Do you think people in Bible times had closer relationships with God than people today have with Him? Explain.**

Get several group members' opinions.

Then say: **Let's take a look at the relationships between God and some famous Bible characters. And let's start with the first two people on earth.**

Have someone read aloud Genesis 1:26, 27; 2:18; 3:8, 9, 21. Then say: **Describe the roles God played in His relationship with Adam and Eve.** (God was their Creator [1:26, 27; 2:18]. He was an accessible friend who talked with them in the garden [3:8, 9]. He was a concerned friend who took care of their needs [3:21].)

Does God fill similar roles in His relationship with us? If so, how? (Yes. God created us; He is accessible to us through prayer; and He meets our needs.) Ask volunteers to give specific examples of how God has taken care of their needs. You may want to be prepared with an example of your own.

Then say: **Now take a look at the relationship between God and Abraham.** Have someone read aloud James 2:23.

Ask: **What one word in this characterizes Abraham's relationship with God?** (Friend.)

What do you think it means to be God's friend? Encourage most of your group members to offer their opinions.

Distribute copies of "God Came Through" (Repro Resource 3). Choose three actors to read the script. While the actors are getting ready, have the rest of the group members review the script because they'll be creating the sound effects (which are indicated by parentheses). You might want to recruit a sound-effects coordinator to stand in front of the group and lead each effect.

After group members have performed the skit once or twice, ask: **How can we tell that God was close to each of these Bible characters?** (He knew what was going on in their lives. He took action to help them.)

What specific actions did He take to help these characters? (He protected Moses when he was a baby, and protected the Israelites from the Egyptians. He helped Joshua and the children of Israel destroy the walls of Jericho. He freed Paul and the others from prison, and He protected Paul and his shipmates during the shipwreck.)

Is God someone we should be scared of? (No. His power is awesome, but He always has people's good at heart.)

Which of the "God Came Through" situations impressed you most, and why? Get several responses.

The Bible is filled with examples of God being close to people. He walked with Adam and Eve in the garden of Eden. He talked to Abraham and even called him "friend." God even came to earth in a human body and lived among people.

Get your group members thinking about how close *they* feel to God. Draw a horizontal line on the board. Instruct group members to men-

tally draw two short vertical lines that intersect it. One line should represent themselves and the other line should represent God. Tell kids to place the two lines close together or far apart based on how close they feel to God.

The King and I

Say: **Maybe you want to get close to God, but not so close that He controls everything you do. You probably don't want to feel confined by God the way that you felt confined when you were nose to nose with your partner at the beginning of this session.**

On the other hand, maybe you feel that God is so powerful, so important, and so holy that people like you and I couldn't possibly be His friends, let alone have any kind of relationship with Him.

Have group members form pairs. Explain that one person in each pair should assume the identity of a famous person from TV, movies, the music industry, the sports world, politics, etc. The other person will be himself or herself. Give the partners a few minutes to come up with common interests or abilities on which they could build a friendship. If they don't know much about the interests of the celebrities they've selected, they can make some up. For example, the partners might both collect baseball cards or enjoy mountain climbing. After the partners have identified common interests, have them discuss how those interests might bring them closer together.

As time permits, find out what interests the members of each pair had in common and how the two could build a friendship.

Ask: **Could you be friends with your partner even though he or she is more famous than you?** (Some group members might agree that common interests could make a friendship possible. Others might feel that they have little grounds for a friendship with a famous person.)

How might a friendship with a famous person be different from a friendship with someone "ordinary," like a friend at school? (You might be more willing to "give" more in a friendship with a famous person because you're in awe of that person. Maybe you would be more respectful to a famous person. You might not act as much like yourself around a famous person as you would around an ordinary friend.)

What similarities do you see between a friendship with God and a friendship with an important person? If someone suggests that a friendship with God might be imbalanced (like a friendship with a famous person) because of the "awe" factor, help him or her see the matter from a different perspective.

Ask: **What do you have in common with God that can bring you close to Him?** (Some of your group members may feel that they have very little in common with God—that they don't understand Him at all or aren't even sure if He exists. Others who are confident in their faith might recognize that they have been made in the likeness of God; that they have the same interests, such as the welfare of loved ones; they both care about the earth; and that they have some of the same characteristics—like the ability to love.)

Explain to your group members that you will be taking a look at Scripture to see how we can be friends with God even though He is infinitely more important and powerful than we are. Acknowledge the "awe" factor and the need to respect God because of His position; but emphasize that God can be a friend and that He is not unreachable, withdrawn, or unknowable.

A Branch in the Vine

(Needed: Bibles, pencils, paper, chalkboard and chalk or newsprint and marker, a plant)

Say: **Just before Jesus' trial and crucifixion, He described to His disciples the kind of close relationship God wants to have with believers.** Have someone read aloud John 15:1-8.

Then ask: **Who is the vine in this illustration?** (The Lord.)

What is our relationship to the vine? (We are branches.)

Distribute paper and pencils. Give group members two minutes to write down as many similarities as they can think of between a branch's relationship with a vine and gardener and our relationship with God. Afterward, have volunteers share their responses. Use the following suggestions to supplement your discussion.

• A vine and its branches usually has a gardener; God is our gardener. He cares for us and looks after us.

• Dead branches must be pruned so that a vine can grow stronger and produce more; God prunes Christians so that we can grow stronger and become more fruitful.

• The branch depends on the vine for life and nourishment so it can bear fruit; we depend on Christ for hope, strength, peace, love, etc.

Ask: **How are we different from a branch?** (We have brains and emotions, so we can be tempted to stop depending on Christ and go off on our own.)

Ask two volunteers to act out the differences between branches and Christians. One should use his or her imagination to play the part of a branch. This person might hug the wall or gently stretch as if in a soft breeze. Encourage the "branch" to ham it up.

The other volunteer should pretend that he or she is involved in a powerful physical struggle against a temptation to sin. This person will demonstrate common spiritual struggles in physical ways.

Explain that the rest of the group members should try to tempt both the "branch" and the Christian to sin by saying things such as "We're going to a crazy party tonight. Wanna come?" or "Wait until you see the magazines my cousin has!" or other things that they know are tempting to Christian teens.

The volunteer portraying the struggling Christian should mime a wrestling match against these invisible temptations and then get on his or her knees and pray. Meanwhile, the branch should wave gently in the breeze (or do whatever branches do), not tempted by anything that is being said. Afterward, thank your volunteers and have them sit down.

Inseparable

(Needed: Bibles)

Introduce the topic of "separation" to your group members. Ask if any of them have ever experienced any kind of separation. If so, ask them to describe how it felt. You may want to use the following questions to focus your discussion.

How did you feel when . . .

• one of your friends moved out of state?

• an older brother or sister left you behind to start college?

• a friend started going out with someone who didn't like you?

• someone you loved died?

• you got lost at a mall or amusement park when you were little?

• you made the team but your best friend didn't?

• the subway door separated you from your family?

• a friend got involved in illegal activities that you didn't participate in?

Let group members share for a while about their experiences. Then acknowledge that separation can be painful and cause us to feel fearful. Separation hurts.

Say: **The good news is that God promises that believers in Christ will never be separated from the love of Christ. Nothing in life or in death can separate us from Christ because of His sacrificial death on the cross, His resurrection, His ascension into heaven, and His constant intercession for us.**

Have someone read aloud Romans 8:35-39. As the person is reading, have the rest of your group members call out things the passage says will *never* separate us from the love of Christ.

Depending on the spiritual maturity of your group members, you may want to read the passage from the Living Bible: "When we have trouble or calamity, when we are hunted down or destroyed . . . if we are hungry, or penniless, or in danger, or threatened with death. . . . For I am convinced that nothing can ever separate us from his love. Death can't, and life can't. The angels won't, and all the powers of hell itself cannot keep God's love away. Our fears for today, our worries about tomorrow, or where we are—high above the sky, or in the deepest ocean—nothing will ever be able to separate us from the love of God demonstrated by our Lord Jesus Christ when he died for us."

As you wrap up the session, distribute balloons to your group members. Have your group members blow up the balloons and tie them.

Then say: **These balloons can remind you of your relationship with God. Think of yourself as the balloon and God as the air inside the balloon. This is how close God wants to be to you. God gives us every breath we take. Job 33:4 says, "The Spirit of God has made me; the breath of the Almighty gives me life." God is as close as your breath—even closer.**

Close the session in prayer, asking God to remind your group members that He wants to have a very close relationship with each of them.

God Came Through

MOSES: The king was killing all baby boys, so my mother hid me on a riverbank *(splash, splash, splash)*. God saw to it that the king's daughter found me and hired my mother to be my nurse *(waah, waah, waah)*. When I grew up, I led the Israelites out of Egypt. The Egyptians followed us with horses *(sound of hoof-beats)*. If they caught us, they were either going to take us back to Egypt *(cries of "No! No!")* or kill us *(sounds of people dying)*. When we came to the Red Sea and had nowhere else to go, things looked hopeless *(dejected cries of "awww")*. But God parted the waters so we could escape *(cheer)*.

JOSHUA: I was chosen to lead Israel *(tramping of feet)* into the Promised Land. God told us to take a fortified city by marching around it for seven days *(tramping of feet)*. On the seventh day, the priests blew trumpets *(ta-dah)* and the walls fell flat *(crash)*.

PAUL: Silas and I were in prison when an earthquake *(rumble, rumble)* freed us. Another time, I was a prisoner being transported by ship when a violent storm came up *(roaring winds, crashing waves)*. The ship was wrecked *(crash, bang)*, but God saved our lives as He promised *(sigh of relief)*.

Step 1
To infuse a bit more action at the beginning of the session, expand the nose-to-nose activity. Depending on your meeting area, you might want to divide into teams and attempt a number of relays (or even race around the outside of the building). Of course, increased activity will likely lead to occasional cheating by not being *completely* nose to nose. To avoid having pairs take too many liberties, you might want to supply lengths of string (or perhaps even Twizzlers) that are about six inches long. Have each member of the pair hold one end in his or her mouth. If either person lets go, or if the string breaks, the pair is disqualified. If you're really brave, let your group members put some creative thought into the possibilities of additional nose-to-nose competitions. They may surprise you with some truly exciting options.

Step 5
Before beginning this step, reacquaint your group with the childhood game "Red Rover." Divide into two teams. The members of one team stand side by side, interlock arms, and challenge one person from the other team to try to break through between any two team members. (You can do away with the chant ["Red rover, red rover, let Billy come over"] if you wish. After all, this is going to be *American Gladiator*-level competition.) Set up a scoring system that provides more points for breaking through between two senior football players as opposed to two junior-high girls. It shouldn't take long playing this game before you're ready to move into the subject of the pain of separation.

Step 4
Sometimes small groups adapt a "second-class citizen" attitude as they compare themselves to large groups who are able to do more things because of significantly larger financial budgets. So to accompany your discussion of the vine and the branches, bring a small clipping from a healthy plant and a pot of dirt to plant it in. Let the clipping serve as on ongoing object lesson. As it grows and flourishes, compare it to your own group. As long as it's from a strong and healthy parent plant, its size is no limitation. It can grow to be just as large and productive as any of its kind. And as group members discover the plant's need for water, fertilizer, proper sunlight, and other nourishment, perhaps they will make the obvious connection to their own growth needs.

Step 5
Another option to help your kids feel better about being a small group is to let them talk about it. Instead of dealing with the individual feelings of separation in this step, let kids discuss how they feel *as a group* about being separated from the large numbers of other Christian kids who go to other churches. The application will be the same: nothing will ever separate them from love of God. He cares every single bit as much for them as for big and glitzy church groups. But if you detect any serious feelings of isolation or regret about not being bigger or able to do everything other groups can do, you might want to spend some time here brainstorming exactly what your group members are looking for. You could even have volunteers contact other church groups in your community or denomination to try to plan some activities that would include several youth groups.

Step 2
In a large group, a lot of people would be left out of the skit on Repro Resource 3 (except for sound effects). So as you hand out copies, ask some of your more biblically knowledgeable people to create additional paragraphs based on other Bible characters for whom "God Came Through" (Daniel, Jonah, Peter walking on water, etc.) Be sure as they write their paragraphs that they also create fun sound effects for the others to do. You'll probably discover that some people have more fun creating their own versions than performing what is already written.

Step 3
The topic of friendship with God can be understood on a cognitive level without actually being felt at a level that changes the behavior of group members. You might want to spend some time explaining that a person's love for God is accurately reflected by his or her love for other people. One common problem with big groups is that shy or somewhat unusual kids can get lost amid all the others without anyone realizing it. Even those who attend every week can come and go without truly being noticed or appreciated. To see if this is happening in your group, give a dollar bill (before the session) to several people you feel may be overlooked. Instruct one person to give the dollar to anyone who asks about his or her school or family life. Another person should give the dollar to anyone who does a favor for him or her. Another might give the dollar to the first person who smiles at him or her. At this point, or perhaps even later in the session, let your volunteers report on whether or not they have given away their dollar bills. Emphasize that we cannot truly consider ourselves friends with God if we are ignoring the needs of the people around us (I John 4:20, 21).

OPTIONS

SESSION TWO

Step 2
Even before you mention God in this session, move from the nose-to-nose activity in Step 1 to a discussion of friendship. Ask: **What characteristics do you look for in a friend? What attracted you to the person who is your best friend? Why are friendships important?** Try to get beyond all the usual answers to things like friends share secrets, friends tell the truth even when it might hurt, friends accept each other as they really are, and so forth. Your "heard it all before" group will expect a follow-up Bible study on relationships or the importance of being a good friend. But you can then resume the session as written and emphasize the privilege of being able to have God as a friend.

Step 4
If your group has a good knowledge of the basic Bible stories and analogies, the vine-and-branches concept might be something they think they fully understand. But you can study the same concept in a different way. Explain that this was written before people knew the secrets of cloning. Ask: **How might a person's spiritual development be compared to becoming a clone?** (We start with a small degree of understanding of who Jesus is and what He has done for us. From there, we attempt to conform ourselves to that image. The more like Him we become, and the less we allow ourselves to be shaped according to our sinful human nature, the more successful we will be.) Ask: **What major "operation(s)" would you need before you could become as good a clone as you know you should be? What else do you need to know about Jesus before you know enough to become a good clone?**

Step 2
This step refers to several different Bible characters, but doesn't go into much detail about any of them. Rather than try to study so many, focus on just one. The "friend of God" concept is a strong one, so you might want to delve into the life of Abraham. Start by letting kids tell you everything they know about Abraham; then fill in other important events of his life from Genesis 12–22: his faithful response to God's call, his association with Lot, the incident with Hagar and Ishmael, the eventual birth of Isaac, and his willingness to offer Isaac back to God. Explain that because of Abraham's long and faithful relationship with God, and the fact that he and God were "friends," Abraham was able to trust God to deliver Isaac on the mountain (Genesis 22). Explain that as we become able to trust God as a friend, He will do great things for each of us as well.

Step 4
The vine-and-branches passage is not easy to understand if it is being read for the first time. Therefore, spend some time discussing it at this point rather than moving directly into the skit. Kids new to this passage need to be able to ask questions about the pruning concept, the emphasis on bearing fruit, and the necessity of an ongoing relationship between the vine and the branches. More importantly, they need to be given a sensitive interpretation of all of the "threatening" portions of this passage: being "cut off" by the gardener (God), being thrown into the fire and burned, etc. At first reading, this passage can sound more scary than encouraging, so don't rush through it. Explain that Jesus' words are strong because He is speaking to His closest friends the day before He is to die. You can then continue the "friends with God" theme to show that His disciples certainly saw themselves as the branches attached to the vine—not the "deadwood" who rejected Jesus. We can be just as confident that Jesus considers us His friends.

Step 2
After you do the "God Came Through" activity on Repro Resource 3, ask group members to complete this sentence: **When I want to draw closer to God, I . . .** You might suggest that Moses went up on Mount Sinai and Daniel prayed three times a day at his window. As your students respond, listen for geographic locations, activities, feelings, and so forth. Later, point out that even though we might feel distant from God, He is always nearby. Rather than seek after a feeling, we need to focus on obeying Him. This is an ideal time to learn to celebrate the friendship between ourselves and God—a bond that Jesus has made possible for us. If you stop to give thanks at this point, it may well be something that your group members will remember sometime in the future when they really *need* a spiritual boost.

Step 4
By this time in the session, you've made passing references to God as friend, king, creator, and vine. Spend some time brainstorming other roles He fills (Father, protector, provider, fair judge, shepherd, etc.). On the board, list all of these roles and what each should mean to us in our ongoing relationship with Him. From time to time, we need to stop and let the importance of these things sink in. You might want to take some time for discussion and sentence prayer at this point to express thanks that we serve a God who is able and willing to attend to our every need. It should not be enough to *know* what God has done. We need to stop and worship Him as well.

Step 2
After reading and discussing "God Came Through" (Repro Resource 3), have group members form teams. Assign each team one or more of the following names of a woman in the Bible and the accompanying references: Hannah (I Samuel 1:26-28); the Shunammite woman (II Kings 4:8-22, 32, 37); Mary, mother of Jesus (Luke 1:28-31); Mary, sister of Lazarus (John 11:32-35, 41-44); Lydia (Acts 16:14, 15); Tabitha (Acts 9:36-42). Ask the teams to read the Bible verses and discuss at least one way we know that God was close to that person. After a few minutes, have each team present its findings to the entire group.

Step 3
At the end of your discussion in this step, ask group members to think about their friendship with God from God's point of view. Ask: **If you were God, more powerful than anyone or anything, how would you feel about being a close friend with a mere human? Since, as God, you would know everything there is to know about your friend, what might you do to improve the friendship?**

Step 3
Most guys can spend the entire meeting time talking about their sports heroes. So when you get to this step, encourage them to cut loose. Ask: **Who are your favorite sports heroes and why? In what ways would you like to be more like the people you admire? How are you most different from those people? Do you think your hero(es) would like to spend a lot of time with you? Do you think you will ever have the same talent, skills, and character of your heroes?** Then shift the discussion to the approachability of God. Ask the same questions in terms of developing a better relationship with Him. Point out that even though the distance between ourselves and God may seem infinitely greater than between ourselves and Michael Jordan, we *can* spend unlimited time with God and become more like Him every day of our lives.

Step 4
Skip the mime exercise, but try to develop the wrestling concept contained in it. For a group of mostly guys, an actual wrestling match is likely to teach a more lasting lesson. (If space is a problem, settle for arm-wrestling.) Select one of your stronger guys and label him the "potential victim." Let others in the group represent temptations of various strengths. Have the "potential victim" take on the first temptation. As soon as that match is over, bring on the next temptation. Don't allow the potential victim much opportunity to rest or regain his strength. If he proves strong enough to master all of the individual temptations, let the temptations begin to attack two at a time. After a while, stop the activity and discuss the vine-and-branches concept again—this time in terms of remaining connected to the Vine for a continual source of strength. Otherwise, our temptations may prove too much for even the strongest of us to master.

Step 1
This session contains passing references to several well-known Bible characters, so you might want to "preview" these characters by singing some favorite songs that pay tribute to these people. For example, you could sing "Father Abraham," "Joshua Fought the Battle of Jericho," "Children, Go Where I Send Thee," "Pharaoh, Pharaoh" (to the tune of "Louie, Louie"), or any other familiar songs about the people mentioned in this session. Or, if your group members are particularly creative, have them write a song that includes all of the characters you mention. (You might be surprised at what your group members can turn out on short notice.)

Step 4
Convert the vine-and-branches analogy into a game. Play by the rules of the pool game "Sharks and Minnows." Designate one person (the vine) to stand in the center of the room. The other group members (useless deadwood) should gather at one end of the room. At your signal, they must run past the vine to the other end of the room. Anyone who is tagged is "grafted," and becomes part of the vine. (They must remain connected.) At your next signal, the deadwood group runs back across the room while the vine members try to tag (graft) more of them. See how long it takes to incorporate all of the people into the vine. If you wish, you can also deal with the real-life applications of this exercise (the powerful effect of evangelism).

MEDIA

Step 2
Rather than leading the group through Repro Resource 3 yourself, pretend to be a movie mogul who is bringing a script to Youth Group Pictures International to be produced. Assign one of the group members to be the director of the picture; then sit back to wait for the "screening." Your director should take responsibility for seeing that all of the functions of filming are taken care of. He or she should find the best actors, see that the lighting is taken care of, and find a good sound-effects crew that will not be content to make the sounds themselves, but will find the right props to create the needed noises. If possible, find a video camera and record the results of your group's "rough cut" of the script.

Step 3
When you begin to discuss the relationships that your young people have with God, give the discussion a media "spin." One option is to ask each person to think of a title of a TV show or movie that best describes his or her relationship with God. ("Who's the Boss?" *Gone with the Wind, Nothing in Common, Bound for Glory,* "Quantum Leap," *Home Alone*, "Three's Company," etc.). Another option is to have group members act out a classic scene that could be applied to their relationship with God (for example, the famous line at the end of *Casablanca*: "I think this is the beginning of a beautiful friendship," or some other meaningful scene from film or television). You're likely to get more quotes from *Revenge of the Nerds* or *Batman Returns* than *The Ten Commandments*, but if kids are honest in their responses, this will be a productive time for them.

Step 1
This session contains many short activities within most of the steps, so you can choose at will. One way to save time is to eliminate Step 2. which is somewhat supplemental to the theme of the session. You can go directly from the questions at the end of Step 1 to the introduction of Step 3. Another shortcut is to emphasize the Bible texts in Steps 4 and 5, and make your own applications. Both the vine-and-branches passage and the "What shall separate us from the love of God?" passage are fairly straightforward. Most group members should be able to find applications to both teachings on their own.

Step 5
If time is extremely tight for you, jump straight from Step 1 to Step 5. The nose-to-nose activity will work well as a lead-in to the reminder that nothing can separate true believers from God's love (Romans 8:35-39). If you then have time for the balloon activity, have kids write down some of the passages on their balloons that they didn't have time to cover during the session (John 15:1-8; James 2:23; etc.). Or challenge them to create slogans to write on their balloons that would help remind them that God is never far away from them.

URBAN

Step 2
Point out that not only is God an accessible friend today, Jesus (when He lived on earth) *chose* people to be His friends and to give Him support during the tough times of His ministry. These friends included many types of people. Help your group members recognize the diversity among the disciples, Jesus' closest friends.
(1) Peter—Bold, trustworthy, hot-tempered.
(2) Andrew—Helpful, eager.
(3) James (of Zebedee)—Active, strong personality.
(4) John—Zealous, strong personality.
(5) James (of Alphaeus)—Faithful to Scripture, Jesus' brother.
(6) Philip—Organizer.
(7) Bartholomew (or Nathanael)—Very intelligent, true Israelite.
(8) Thomas—Investigator, risk-taker.
(9) Matthew—Detailed, picky, tax collector.
(10) Simon (the Zealot)—Committed to a cause, wanted little to do with the government.
(11) Judas Iscariot—Untrustworthy, betrayed Jesus.
(12) Thaddaeus (or James)—Quiet.

Have group members decide which disciple's personality is similar to their own. Then read aloud John 15:13-16. Encourage group members to choose Jesus as their personal friend as Jesus chooses them as His personal friends.

Step 4
Rather than having volunteers mime the branch and the person facing temptation, you might want to have them simulate a boxing match in which a fighter "battles" various temptations.

Step 3
Junior highers are usually better able to deal with tangible things than with conceptual ideas. Many of them are also enthusiastic about science and nature subjects. So as you discuss topics such as closeness to God and the development of a friendship with Him, here's a way to do it in both a tangible and "scientific" way. Set up a solar system in your room, with the sun at one end and the planets (Mercury, Venus, Earth, Mars, Jupiter, Saturn, Uranus, Neptune, and Pluto) at intervals out from the sun. Also designate a far corner of the room as "the other side of the galaxy." Explain that God's presence is represented by the sun. Then instruct kids to stand in the appropriate places in response to each of the following questions:

- **Where would you say you are now in your relationship with God?**
- **Where would you say most people your age are?**
- **Where do you think the most comfortable place for you would be?**
- **Where do you think God wants you to be?**
- **What's the closest you've ever been to God?**
- **What's the farthest away you've ever been?**

Then discuss why kids are more distant than they want to be, what causes them to draw near or move away from God, etc.

Step 5
Rather than discussing how nothing can separate us from God's love, junior highers might be more inclined to need some motivation to *start* a personal relationship with Him. If possible, bring in some samples of good devotional materials. If group members find something that seems promising, encourage them to invest in the book as a first step in their ongoing spiritual development. Later, after they've dealt with the basics of their relationship with God, they will be more prepared to deal with the assurance that nothing can separate them from God's love.

Step 2
A group that is ready for a deeper-than-average level of study might appreciate a different twist on the "God Came Through" activity on Repro Resource 3. Have group members form teams. Instruct the teams to study ways that God comes through even when He chooses not to deliver His people right away. For example, one team might look at Job (Job 1–2; 42). Another might study Jesus' trial and crucifixion (Matthew 27; Luke 23; John 19). Yet another might examine the ongoing sufferings of Paul (II Corinthians 11). Have all of the teams discuss how personal suffering may indeed be one way that God "comes through," even though we may not realize it at the time. Conclude by looking as a group at Romans 5:3-5 to see how our ultimate hope in God is rooted in our sufferings.

Step 5
Ask group members to write their own, personalized versions of Romans 8:35-39. They may not be able to relate well to persecution, famine, nakedness, danger, or sword; but most of them are well aware of other threats such as sexual temptation, intense pressures to excel, financial shortcomings, and so forth. Each person should insert his or her own spiritual struggles into the passage. Let volunteers read what they've written, but don't force anyone to do so. Encourage group members to hang on to these paraphrases and pull them out during times when they feel as if no one understands what they're going through.

Date Used:

Approx. Time

Step 1: Too Close for Comfort _____
o Extra Action
o Extra Fun
o Short Meeting Time
Things needed:

Step 2: Voices from the Past _____
o Large Group
o Heard It All Before
o Little Bible Background
o Fellowship & Worship
o Mostly Girls
o Media
o Urban
o Extra Challenge
Things needed:

Step 3: The King and I _____
o Large Group
o Mostly Girls
o Mostly Guys
o Media
o Combined Junior High/High School
Things needed:

Step 4: A Branch in the Vine _____
o Small Group
o Heard It All Before
o Little Bible Background
o Fellowship & Worship
o Mostly Guys
o Extra Fun
o Urban
Things needed:

Step 5: Inseparable _____
o Extra Action
o Small Group
o Short Meeting Time
o Combined Junior High/High School
o Extra Challenge
Things needed:

SESSION

3 If God Speaks, Why Can't I Hear Him?

YOUR GOALS FOR THIS SESSION:

Choose one or more

- ☐ To help kids recognize the different ways God communicates with them.
- ☐ To help kids understand reasons why they may not "hear" God.
- ☐ To help kids make changes in their lives so that they can hear God better.
- ☐ Other ______________________________

Your Bible Base:

I Kings 9:11-13
John 4:24; 10:1-5
I Thessalonians 5:23

Speak to Me!

OPTIONS

Have group members form pairs. Then have each pair choose another pair to compete with. The members of each pair will stand back to back, with the backs of their heads touching. Each set of competing pairs will stand next to each other.

Designate one person in each pair to be the "sender," and the other to be the "receiver." The object of the game is for the sender to communicate a message to his or her partner (the receiver) without being heard by the members of the competing pair. Group members may not move or even turn their heads during the activity.

The first pair to successfully communicate its message without being heard by its opponent wins.

Afterward, ask: **Which is harder, communicating back to back or face to face? Explain.** (Communicating back to back is harder because we often depend on sight to communicate. Making gestures and facial expressions is an important part of the communication process.)

Explain: **Some people find it hard to talk to God because they can't see Him. Other people say they find it hard to talk to God because they can't hear God speak to them. Have you ever felt this way?** Encourage several group members to respond honestly.

Imagine asking someone all kinds of questions or telling that person all kinds of personal secrets and never getting any kind of response. It would be very frustrating. Yet some people feel this is what it's like when they talk to God. They feel as if they never get a response. So they give up. If you've ever felt this way, today's session is for you.

STEP 2

I Can't Understand You

(Needed: Three index cards prepared according to instructions, large marshmallows, dinner roll, banana, paper, pencils)

Have group members form three teams. Instruct each team to choose a representative (preferably someone who is hungry). Give the representatives what you think are equal amounts of food. You should give each representative enough food to fill up his or her mouth. You might give one person three large marshmallows; you might give another a small dinner roll; and you might give the other half of a banana.

Also give each representative an index card with the following message written on it: *Isn't it frustrating when your mom calls to you from another room and tells you something important, but you can't quite hear what she said? So you yell, "What?" And she says it again, but you still can't hear her. The best way to solve this problem is to move closer to each other. Then you'll be able to communicate better.*

Distribute paper and pencils to the rest of the team members. Explain to the representatives that they are to stuff the food in their mouths (no chewing allowed) and read aloud from the cards you gave them. [NOTE: Emphasize caution on the part of your representatives. Don't have them put so much food in their mouths that they run a risk of choking.]

The first team to figure out and write down exactly what its representative is saying wins. When a team has figured out the message, the representative may swallow or spit out the food.

Afterward, focus on the message communicated by the representatives—particularly on the idea of "moving closer" to facilitate communication.

Say: **The same solution applies to people who are having trouble hearing what God is saying to them. In a sense, they've got to move closer to God. Then they will be able to hear Him better.**

More Than One Way

(Needed: Bibles, Repro Resource 4, paper, pencils)

OPTIONS

Say: **Let's take a look at some ways God spoke to people in the past.** Distribute copies of "How God Spoke" (Repro Resource 4) and pencils. Have kids work in pairs to unscramble the words on the sheet.

The answers are as follows:

(1) ANGEL in a VISION—An angel interpreted a vision for Zechariah. Zechariah found out that God would bless His people (Zechariah 1:8-17).

(2) THREE MEN appeared to Abraham to announce that his wife would have a son (Genesis 18:1, 2, 10).

(3) BURNING BUSH—God's voice came from a fiery bush to tell Moses that God would rescue the Israelites from slavery (Exodus 3:1-8).

(4) WRITING on the WALL—God sent a hand that wrote a message on a wall telling King Belshazzar that he would die (Daniel 5).

(5) DONKEY—God let Balaam's donkey speak, which helped save a disobedient Balaam from being destroyed by God (Numbers 22:1, 4-6, 21-33).

(6) ANOTHER MAN—Gad was told by God to tell David to build an altar (II Samuel 24:18, 19).

(7) God told Paul through HIS SPIRIT that people will abandon the faith (I Timothy 4:1).

(8) God spoke to our forefathers through the PROPHETS (Hebrews 1:1).

(9) In these last days, God has spoken to us through HIS SON (Hebrews 1:2).

After you go through the answers, discuss which methods of communication were most bizarre, which ones might have been frightening, which messages brought good news, which ones brought bad news, whether the people who received the messages were obedient or not, etc.

Have group members remain in their pairs. Give each pair a pencil and paper. Then say: **Imagine that one of you needs directions from the other on how to get to the new video store. But the person giving direction has laryngitis, and can't talk at all. List as many different ways as you can think of for communicating the directions without talking.** After a minute or two, ask volunteers to share their ideas. Answers might include writing out directions, using sign language, miming the answer, finding someone else to help, taking the person to the store yourself, etc.

Say: **As you've discovered, there are other ways to communicate besides using audible words.** Talk about how God communicates with us today and if His methods are anything like ours. (For instance, we write directions for each other; God wrote directions for us in the Bible. God doesn't use sign language, but He does "show" us things about Himself through His creation. God also communicates to us through pastors and other Christians.)

Have you ever heard someone say, "God told me," or "God spoke to me"? What you think people mean by these phrases? Point out that while God *can* use an audible voice to speak to us, more often than not He communicates in other ways. Most often, He speaks to us through the Bible.

Say: **There is one other unique way in which God can communicate to us.** Have someone read aloud John 4:24.

Then ask: **What does "God is spirit" mean?** (He is invisible and without a flesh-and-blood body like ours.)

Have someone read aloud I Thessalonians 5:23. Ask: **What three aspects of a human being are mentioned here?** (Spirit, soul, and body.)

Explain: **God is a spirit. When He created us, He gave us a spirit so we would be like Him and, therefore, could communicate with Him. So, one of the important ways God talks to us is silently, in our spirit, in an inaudible voice.**

If your group members seem confused by this, or want further clarification, have them look up Romans 8:16, which says, "The [Holy] Spirit . . . testifies with our spirit that we are God's children." In ways we can't put into words, God can assure us inwardly that we belong to Him.

Listen Up!

(Bibles, tape recording of familiar voices, tape player)

Have someone read aloud I Kings 19:11-13. Then ask: **What does this passage say about the way the Lord speaks to us?** (Rather than using some dramatic and powerful wind, earthquake, or fire, God

speaks to us in a "gentle whisper.")

To demonstrate this, have a volunteer stand in front of the group and read aloud Psalm 23 while several other volunteers talk loudly.

Afterward, ask: **How well could you hear God's Word being spoken to you amidst all the noise and talking?** (Probably not very well.)

That's one reason why Christians are not always able to hear God's silent inner voice: There's too much going on. We get too busy; our lives are too noisy to hear God's voice.

Have group members sit for one minute in complete silence and ask them to listen for as many background sounds as they can hear.

Afterward, ask: **What sounds could you hear when it was silent?** (The sounds of traffic, the heater or air conditioner, a dog barking, breathing, etc.)

In which situation would it be easier to hear God's inner voice—the first situation or the second? Most group members will probably agree on the second.

What percent of your waking day would you describe as very noisy? Somewhat noisy? Somewhat quiet? Very quiet?

Have someone read aloud John 10:1-5. Explain that in this illustration Jesus compares us to sheep and Himself to the Shepherd. He speaks to His own—that's us Christians. He knows us personally and communicates personally to us. We can hear Him because we're listening (vs. 3). We know His voice and can tell it from a stranger's (vs. 4, 5).

Play a tape recording of voices familiar to your group members. Have your group members try to identify the voices.

Then ask: **Why were you able to identify the voices?** (We know the people or have heard them a lot. The voices are distinctive from everyone else's.)

Have a volunteer reread John 10:4. Explain: **It's pretty easy to recognize the voice of someone you know well or someone you've watched a lot. The same applies to hearing God's voice. The more that we get to know God, the better we will recognize His voice. His silent inner voice will become familiar to us when He communicates to us through a Scripture passage, through another Christian, through a life experience, or silently in our spirit.**

Seeing Me

(Needed: Copies of Repro Resource 5)

Distribute copies of "Hearing God" (Repro Resource 5). Give group members a few minutes to complete the sheet. For #6, have them draw their own pictures. When they're finished, ask volunteers to share their responses.

Answers might include the following: (1) It's too noisy. (2) She doesn't have enough time. (3) She's too busy. (4) They're not listening. (5) He's not paying attention.

Briefly discuss each scenario, asking your group members how big of a problem they think each one is in most kids' relationships with God.

Then say: **Look at the scenarios again. Write a "1" next to the one that you need to work on first. Then write a "2" next to the one you need to work on next, etc.**

Before you close the session in prayer, give group members a minute of silence so they can ask God to help them work on their #1 priority so they'll be better able to hear Him. Also, challenge your kids to spend more time reading God's Word. As they do, they will be more likely to really hear Him.

How GOD Spoke

Unscramble the following words to find out how God spoke to people in the past. Then look up the passage to see who He was speaking to and what He said.

1. **GALNE in a SIVNIO** (Zechariah 1:8-17)
2. **RETEH ENM** (Genesis 18:1, 2, 10)
3. **UBNIGNR HUSB** (Exodus 3:1-8)
4. **TGNWIRI on the LWLA** (Daniel 5)
5. **KDEOYN** (Numbers 22:1, 4-6, 21-33)
6. **RETOHNA NMA** (II Samuel 24:18, 19)
7. **HSI IITPSR** (I Timothy 4:1)
8. **OHSTPPRE** (Hebrews 1:1)
9. **SHI SNO** (Hebrews 1:2)

Hearing God

1. Reason he may not be able to hear God:

2. Reason she may not be able to hear God:

3. Reason she may not be able to hear God:

4. Reason they may not be able to hear God:

5. Reason he may not be able to hear God:

6. Reason this person may not be able to hear God:

Step 3
When you get ready for Repro Resource 4, don't hand out copies as instructed. Instead, use the various methods God uses to communicate with us as clues for a Pictionary-type drawing activity. Divide group members into teams. Have one person from each team come to the front of the room and look at the clue (angel, vision, burning bush, writing on the wall, donkey, etc.) he or she is to draw. Then the players should return to their teams and, at your signal, begin to draw. Drawers are not allowed to write words, numbers, or symbols. They must simply attempt to draw the image they are assigned. Don't tell them what the common theme is, but let them try to figure it out after they've done a few drawings. Some of the methods on the sheet may need to be adapted for this type of activity. (For example, you might want to have kids draw "companion" rather than "another man"). But at the end of the exercise you can clarify how each drawing represents a different means of God's communication to us.

Step 4
As a variation of discussing how we are like sheep and Jesus is like a shepherd, have someone lead a quick game of Simon Says. The leader should begin with simple commands, and then increase the pace and the difficulty. (Go from "Simon says raise your hands" to "Simon says don't refuse to keep your hands up.") After many people have been eliminated, discuss why they messed up when they were intentionally listening so closely. (Didn't understand the instruction? Didn't pay attention for a moment? Imitated the movement of someone else?) Then move into the sheep-shepherd relationship discussion as you explain that sheep are also easily confused and must listen very closely to the voice of the shepherd or they stand to get in a lot of trouble.

Step 1
Members of a small group might know each other too well to need to guess partners or find out additional information about others. So take a different approach to show the benefits of face-to-face communication. Ask one person to volunteer to tell about his or her day at school. The others should listen; but before they do, give each person a slip of paper that contains an imaginary situation that would influence the level of interest he or she has in the speaker. Situations might include the following:

• Your dad just had a heart attack this morning and his condition is still unstable.
• You have a massive crush on the person who is speaking.
• The speaker's father owns a company that needs a summer worker. You want the job because it's easy, and pays better than anything in town.
• You've stayed up the past two nights cramming for exams—and you still failed.

The speaker should get quite a variety of nonverbal responses based on facial expressions of the listeners. Afterward, have him or her describe the speaking experience. Was he or she annoyed by any of the audience's responses? Did he or she think some of the listeners cared more than others about what he or she had to say? Explain that sometimes the situations we face may prevent us from "hearing" God when He communicates to us.

Step 2
With a small group, you have the ability to give *everybody* a mouthful of food, rather than just choosing three volunteers. And instead of using a "script," have group members try to carry on a regular conversation. Try to keep the conversation light and humorous, because the more you can get them laughing, the more effective the food will be as a distortion device. If you want to add an additional challenge, put more distance between the kids. It may be a challenge to see which they project farther: their voices or food particles.

Step 4
Sometimes the more people who get involved in the communication process, the less effective their efforts become. Divide your large group into three or four teams. Blindfold one person per team. Hide a small item somewhere in the room where everyone (except the blindfolded people) can see it. Then spin the blindfolded people enough for them to lose their bearings and give a signal to begin. Each team should try to direct its blindfolded member to the hidden item by giving *only the following directions*: "left," "right," "forward," "behind you," "up," or "down." When everyone begins this process at once, it will cause quite a commotion—one that isn't likely to be helpful to the blindfolded people. Smart teams will discover that they should appoint only one person to give directions, but see how long it takes them to find this out.

Step 5
Since you have a lot of people on hand, let them adapt Repro Resource 5 into roleplays rather than just still art. Challenge everyone to make the situations "come alive" by providing personal experiences wherever possible. Feel free to adapt them if you want to, or let kids come up with additional situations of their own. You should still discuss the reasons the people may be unable to hear God in each case. You should also have kids follow up the roleplays with a priority list of which situations they most need to work on.

Step 3

Instruct group members to sit in a circle. Have each person in turn mention a method that God uses to communicate with people. Make an elimination game of it. When one person is unable to answer, he or she is "out"; continue until you get down to a single person. Before beginning, make sure kids understand that any biblical example is OK to use. So while God rarely uses burning bushes today, it's still a valid example because He used one with Moses. But don't provide *too much* leeway. All answers must be valid historic or current means of communication. While God *could* certainly choose to manipulate clouds into spelling out "I want you to become a missionary," this answer would not count unless it had actually happened to someone. When everyone is out, see how well your group members did by having them complete Repro Resource 4.

Step 4

The image of Jesus as shepherd and Christians as sheep is quite common. Your heard-it-all-before group might be quick to write it off as just another Bible cliché. If they don't appreciate it, have them come up with something better. Tell them you understand the difficulty of cool kids like them relating to antiquated agricultural images like the one in John 10:1-5. Then ask each person to come up with a "new and improved" analogy that would make the same point. It needs to be something that most people can relate to in their own relationship with Jesus—simple and universal. Group members are likely to discover that it's harder than it seems to create effective analogies. They might come up with things like CEO/employees, coach/team members, day-care leader/little kids, etc.

Step 3

Repro Resource 4 could be intimidating to people who don't know much about Scripture. While the unscrambling should go fine, looking up the verses and trying to understand what's going on in each case might be much more confusing. Dismembered hands writing on walls, talking donkeys, angels, and visions are all amazing and mysterious events which may become overwhelming when combined into a single activity. It will probably be far more helpful if you lead a group discussion about one or two of the main stories instead. The story of Balaam is a tough one for people new to the Bible to understand, so you could help them understand the events of the story that led to the talking donkey. The burning bush, on the other hand, is a story that most kids can deal with on their own because the events are clear and easy to understand. You know your group better than anyone else, so cover the stories you think would be most beneficial to them.

Step 4

In contrast with the earlier references to burning bushes, talking donkeys, and other miraculous signs, you might expect a bit of confusion when you get to the passage in I Kings 19:11-13. A logical question might arise at this point, especially from someone not well versed in Bible teaching. If not, you should ask it yourself: **Since God is able to perform any powerful and wonderful sign He wishes, why in the world does He ever choose to speak in a "gentle whisper"?** Let kids offer answers. They should eventually come to the conclusion that God almost always provides us with a choice of whether or not we hear and/or obey. His preference is usually two-way communication (like father to child or friend to friend) rather than dictatorial shows of force. We need to remember that He is always able to express Himself in powerful and perhaps frightening ways, but He shouldn't always *need* to in order to capture our attention.

Step 4

As a group, create a "covenant to listen." We may not think in terms of listening as being a worship activity, yet it is an important part of any person's relationship with God. So try to think of a number of things your group members will agree to do individually as they strive for spiritual maturity. Structure your covenant any way you wish. One option, however, would be to begin with a section of *confession.* ("We talk too much and don't listen enough." "Our quiet times are not usually quiet enough.") Then write a section of *appreciation* for God's patience with us and all He has done and continues to do. Finally, conclude with a section of *intention*—what your members will agree to change in the future to improve their relationships with God.

Step 5

Too often, closing prayers are taken for granted. Some young people tend not to give them adequate thought or attention. In this case, if time permits, make your closing prayer more of a worship activity. First, challenge each group member to mentally complete this sentence: **Because God speaks _____________, I will _____________.** Give some examples. ("Because God speaks softly, I will make more of an effort to have a regular quiet time to listen for Him." "Because God speaks clearly, I will do whatever He tells me to do.") Then close with sentence prayers. Encourage each person to participate. The listening covenant (from the "Fellowship & Worship" option for Step 4) is a group commitment, but when it comes to listening for God's voice, the responsibility must be up to each individual.

Step 4
After you discuss I Kings 19:11-13, ask your group members if they know someone who is hearing impaired. Discuss any experiences they've had. Talk about the adjustments a hearing-impaired person must make and what things might help to aid in communication with such a person.

Step 5
After completing "Hearing God" (Repro Resource 5), ask your group members to use the back of the resource sheet to write a brief schedule of one day in the previous week. Then have them consider how important it is to them to hear God's voice. Ask: **What can you shorten or eliminate in your daily schedule in order to have time that is quiet enough for you to listen to God?** Ask some volunteers to discuss possible options.

Step 2
Guys are usually pretty competitive, so make more of a contest out of the food exercise. Keep the three volunteers who cram food in their mouths, but assign each of these people a team and a list of instructions to call out to their team members (who should be standing a far distance away). The instructions you hand to one person might read: "Your team members are Bill, John, Chad, Taj, and Simon. You are to instruct Bill to hop up and down on his right foot. John should stand with his hand on his head. Chad should sit on the floor. Taj should 'assume the position' against the wall as if he were being arrested. And Simon should turn toward the wall and look at you over his shoulder." The list of team members and their assigned commands should be different for each of the three volunteers. When the exercise begins, no one should know which of the three people is on his team. At your signal, the three volunteers will simultaneously try to outshout each other and be the first to have all of his team members acting according to instructions.

Step 3
Have guys pair up. Ask each pair to demonstrate one way that guys indicate that they like or admire each other. It's no easy task to appear manly and expressive at the same time, and many guys have quite a system worked out. Pairs should be able to think of a number of ways: high fives, special handshakes, a pat on the back, a thumbs-up signal, a punch on the arm, and so forth. Tie this exercise in with the session's discussion of how, since God is spirit, we have a special way of relating to Him as well. You might also want to point out that guys who are good friends tend to be able to be in each other's presence for hours at a time without necessarily feeling the need to say anything. This observation can tie in to the need for periods of quiet in the time we spend with God.

Step 3
A good game to accompany the introduction to nonverbal communication is "Peep, Peep." Have everyone sit in a circle except for one blindfolded person who sits in the center of the circle. Spin the center person around and have him or her walk until he or she bumps into one of the seated people. He or she should then sit in the lap of (or stand next to) the person and say, "Peep, peep." The person should respond in the same manner, though may change his or her voice to try to prevent being recognized. The blindfolded person can say "Peep, peep" up to three times and have the other person respond. Then he or she must guess who the person is. If he or she is correct, the other person goes to the center. If not, the blindfolded person returns to the center and tries again. You can use this activity to point out that as we begin to deal with unusual forms of communication, they may be hard to get used to at first. It may be difficult to understand God's "inaudible voice" if we aren't accustomed to listening for it.

Step 4
When you deal with familiar voices during this step, an additional observation to make is that sometimes familiar voices cannot be trusted. Call for volunteers, four at a time. One should be blindfolded. One should have a prize of some kind (dollar bill, candy bar, etc.). One should have some kind of penalty (squirt gun, water balloon, etc.). The last person has neither prize nor penalty. At your signal, all three people try to convince the blindfolded person to choose them. They can promise, lie, threaten, or do whatever they wish to sway the person's decision. When the person chooses, he or she gets whatever the person is holding. Explain that this demonstrates why it is so important to learn to hear God's gentle voice. We hear a lot of advice and promises; sometimes the number of voices confuses us. God, however, will never lie to or mislead us.

Step 3

Rather than using Repro Resource 4 as an unscrambling exercise, use it as a basis for news reports instead. Let kids form news teams and choose one of the examples to research and report on. In each case, the teams should lead off with, "Our top story tonight—God speaks!" Encourage them to "ham it up." For example, one or two people could be seated at the anchor desk and "go live to the scene" where other kids give on-the-spot reports. They might simply report the facts, or they might interview the character(s) involved. Afterward, you can do a "recap" that includes all of the methods the teams chose as well as the others on the sheet.

Step 5

After you finish Repro Resource 5, say: **Suppose you had a message you wanted to take to all of the other people your age and an unlimited budget to spend. How would you go about reaching the most people? What types of media would you use? Within those categories of media, what specific ones would you target?** (If television, which shows? If magazine advertising, which magazines?) Have kids share their plans with each other. Then ask: **With all of these possibilities, why does God still use a gentle whisper to speak to the hearts of individuals?** Wait for students to respond. Some may comment on the frequent misrepresentations of a few TV preachers. Some might realize that what is basically an entertainment medium is not an effective channel for deep spiritual truth or personal development. Others are sure to have their own unique observations. But all should appreciate the easy (and perpetual) accessibility of God in our lives. We never have to worry about having "the cable go out" or having our "subscription canceled."

Step 3

Begin the session with the Repro Resource 4 activity, but focus only on the ways God has used to communicate with people. Let kids take their sheets home to look up the verses and see who God spoke to and what He said. The tape-recorded exercise in Step 4 can be eliminated. And you can plan on making Repro Resource 5 optional. If time permits, the sheet is a good way to end the session. If not, however, you can close in Step 4 after reading John 10:1-5. Challenge your young people to learn to identify the voice of God in their lives and to trust whatever He has to say. Otherwise, they are liable to follow some voices that don't have their best interests in mind.

Step 4

If your time is very limited for this session, your kids shouldn't have a problem drawing applications directly from the two main Bible passages. Divide into two teams. Have the first team read and discuss I Kings 19:11-13. Have the second team read and discuss John 10:1-5. Have the teams prepare to report what they discover about hearing and responding to God's voice. Challenge them to "read between the lines" and deal with inferences and applications in addition to the obvious answers that are contained there. Since these passages are short, the teams should have time to "spin off" into several related areas and ideas. Close by having everyone complete Repro Resource 5 and determine which of the areas he or she needs to work on first.

Step 1

Try another activity to help young people put the noise of their lives in perspective. Have group members form pairs. Give one person in each pair a slip of paper that reads, "The lively liver of London lies lonely in the laboratory." Give the other person a piece of paper and a pencil. Instruct the first person in each pair to read his or her message once. The object of the activity is for the second person to write down what he or she hears the first person say. Sounds easy, huh? It's not. Bring in a large tape player or radio and play some extremely loud music. Also, the pairs should stand back to back for the activity. Give the pairs a minute to complete the assignment; then see how well some of them do. Try a second round, with the members of the pairs standing face to face, and with no music at all. The pairs will probably find the second round to be much easier than the first one. If you wish, repeat the activity using another phrase. Afterward, point out that "noise" in our lives can lessen our ability to understand God's "gentle whisper" in our hearts and minds.

Step 5

Integrate into the activity this question: **What words would the people in this city hear from God if they took time to listen?**

Step 3

The instructions in this step are to "imagine" a problem that involves the inability to communicate verbally. But junior highers will get more involved if they can act out situations rather than imagining them. So give a few volunteers some instructions to try to communicate to other people in nonverbal ways. Here are a few for starters:

- "You're in danger. Come with me."
- "I think you're cuter than anyone else in this room."
- "Do you want to go to your house for a Coke and to study math?"

This activity should lead right into the discussion on God's use of nonaudible communication.

Step 4

The value of silence may best be appreciated by going to the other extreme. Junior highers usually don't have a problem being loud, so challenge them to see just how good they are at it. Divide into four teams (or two, for smaller groups) and conduct a shouting contest. Start with two of the teams competing for volume as well as sustained noise. Determine a winner and then let the other two teams compete. Determine the winner there and have the finals between the two winning teams. You may not accomplish a lot with this activity, but it's a lot of fun. And in addition, many of the members will welcome the opportunity to sit quietly and listen to you for a while after going all-out in this kind of competition.

Step 3

The fact that God doesn't always try to overpower us with His "voice" lends itself to some creative discussions. Ask: **Does this mean that we have the choice and/or the ability to overpower God?** Let kids comment. They should eventually reach the conclusion that, in fact, we can block out God's voice if we don't attempt to "tune in" to what He wants to tell us. However, that doesn't mean He won't continue with His plans. It simply means we're in the dark about what's going on—and we could face potentially dangerous situations—if we don't listen for His leading. Have volunteers read aloud Ephesians 4:30 and I Thessalonians 5:19. Based on these verses, it seems clear that we are able to both "grieve" the Spirit of God and quench the Spirit (or, "put out the Spirit's fire," according to NIV.) But in both cases, we are instructed to avoid these things. While we may be able to ignore what God is trying to tell us, it is never wise to do so.

Step 5

As an alternative to Repro Resource 5, ask your group members to construct "Daily Noise Pie Charts." Using a circle to represent a day's worth of conscious time (not including time asleep), they should determine an average of how much time they spend listening to various things. Some of these things might include "forced listening" (such as classes at school or similar settings), conversations, TV, radio/ Walkmans, music on their stereos, and so forth. As they fill out their charts, they should also determine what percentage of each day involves pure, complete silence. Some of your members might discover that if hearing God's voice requires a totally quiet and isolated setting, maybe He's not getting through because He rarely has a good opportunity. If so, let each person determine how he or she might rearrange the percentages and leave more time devoted to listening for God's voice.

Date Used:

Approx. Time

Step 1: Speak to Me! ______
o Small Group
o Urban
Things needed:

Step 2: I Can't Understand You ______
o Small Group
o Mostly Guys
Things needed:

Step 3: More Than One Way ______
o Extra Action
o Heard It All Before
o Little Bible Background
o Mostly Guys
o Extra Fun
o Media
o Short Meeting Time
o Combined Junior High/High School
o Extra Challenge
Things needed:

Step 4: Listen Up! ______
o Extra Action
o Large Group
o Heard It All Before
o Little Bible Background
o Fellowship & Worship
o Mostly Girls
o Extra Fun
o Short Meeting Time
o Combined Junior High/High School
Things needed:

Step 5: Seeing Me ______
o Large Group
o Fellowship & Worship
o Mostly Girls
o Media
o Urban
o Extra Challenge
Things needed:

SESSION 4

How Does the Holy Spirit "Live" in Me?

YOUR GOALS FOR THIS SESSION:

Choose one or more

☐ To help kids recognize that the Holy Spirit lives in them if they're Christians.

☐ To help kids understand the roles the Holy Spirit wants to fill in their lives.

☐ To help kids discover what the Holy Spirit will and will not do for them and how to allow Him to work in them.

☐ Other ______________________________

____

Your Bible Base:

John 14:15-27
I Corinthians 6:19

Tricked!

(Needed: Coin, paper of various sizes)

Begin the session by having your group members try to perform a few impossible stunts. However, don't tell group members that the stunts are impossible until after they've attempted them.

First, ask a volunteer to stand with his or her heels against the wall. Set a coin on the floor in front of the person about two feet away. Have the person reach for the coin, keeping his or her heels against the wall. He or she may not hold on to anyone or anything in reaching for the coin. When he or she fails, ask for other volunteers to attempt it.

Next, hand a sheet of paper to one of your group members. Instruct him or her to fold the paper in half ten times. When he or she fails, ask for other volunteers to attempt it. Give them various sizes of paper to try to fold. Folding any size sheet of paper ten times is impossible.

Next, walk up to one of your group members (preferably one who is the same sex you are) and say: **I'm the leader; you're the follower. I can find a place to sit in this room that you can't sit in.** Sit down on the floor. Then get up, and invite the follower to sit on the floor too. Then sit on a chair in the room, get up, and invite the follower to sit on the chair too. Before the follower has a chance to stand up again, quickly sit on his or her lap. This proves the point of the activity: The follower can't sit on his or her own lap. (The ideas for these stunts came from *I Bet I Can: I Bet You Can't* by E. Richard Churchill [Sterling Publications Co., 1982].)

Ask group members if they know any similar tricks. If they do, let them demonstrate—if the tricks are appropriate for your group.

Afterward, say: **OK, I admit it, these were simple stunts. But were some of these outcomes easier to predict than others?**

What's the most baffling magic trick you've ever seen? Get a few responses.

Besides stunts and magic tricks, what are some other things in life that are hard to figure out? (Group members may list things like algebra, science, how to stay out of trouble, the opposite sex, the Bible, parents or siblings, evil, etc.) List group members' responses on the board as they are named.

If group members didn't mention "the Bible" on their list, add it yourself. Then say: **Many people think the Bible is difficult to understand. They say there are doctrines, events, and people**

in it that are hard to figure out. One of these hard-to-understand teachings is the concept of the Holy Spirit living inside of Christians. It's no stunt, illusion, or trick; it's a fact.

Try to remember back to the first time you heard this teaching about the Holy Spirit living in believers. Did you find it hard to believe or understand? How did you feel about it? Some group members may say that it was hard to imagine that God Himself would come to live inside someone once he or she became a Christian. Perhaps it was hard for them to think of a holy God in contact with a sinner.

Say: **It's important to understand and believe the teaching of God living in us, so we're going to investigate this biblical truth in this session.**

STEP 2

An Awesome Fact

Ask: **Which is easier to believe: that God would live in a building or in a person?** Get several responses, if possible.

Then explain that God actually *did* choose to focus His manifested presence in a building at one time. It was the temple that the Israelites built. But after Jesus died on the cross and was resurrected from the dead, God sent the Holy Spirit to live in every person who received Jesus as Savior (Romans 8:9).

Have someone read aloud I Corinthians 6:19. Then ask: **How are we like the building the Israelites built?** (We are temples too, because God lives in us.)

Explain: **Whether we feel God or not, the fact is that when we genuinely invite Jesus to be our Savior, the Holy Spirit does come to live in us. The Holy Spirit's presence can bring about great changes in our lives. In other words, the One who *resides* in our lives wants to *preside* over our lives.**

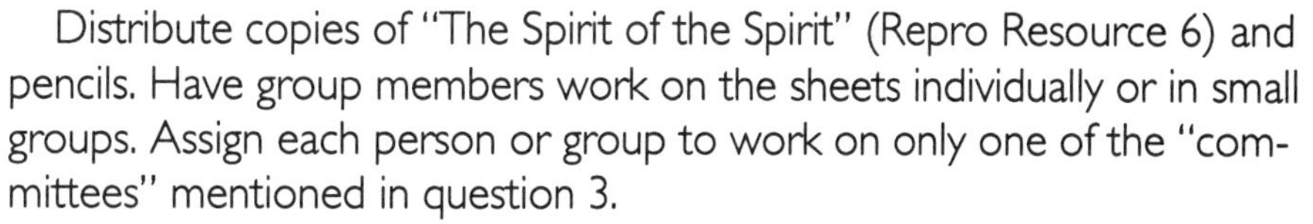

Meet the Holy Spirit

(Needed: Bibles, copies of Repro Resource 6, pencils)

Distribute copies of "The Spirit of the Spirit" (Repro Resource 6) and pencils. Have group members work on the sheets individually or in small groups. Assign each person or group to work on only one of the "committees" mentioned in question 3.

Give your group members a few minutes to work. When they're finished, ask volunteers to share their responses. Use the following information to supplement group members' answers.

(1) Jesus promised to ask God to send the Holy Spirit (vs. 16). The Holy Spirit will stay forever (vs. 16). Jesus wouldn't leave us as orphans, but came to us through the Holy Spirit (vs. 18). The Holy Spirit is God because He replaces Jesus on earth (vss. 16-18). The Holy Spirit will make His home with us (vs. 23). The Holy Spirit will teach us and remind us of Jesus' words (vs. 26).

(2) Counselor—One who gives aid and comfort; Spirit of Truth—One who shows what's right in all areas; Guide—One who shows the way; Teacher—One who instructs.

(3) *Committee #1: Most Helpful Person of the Year*—One who is always there for you; one who offers help, but doesn't take over or force his or her way on you; one who is willing to do hard things if necessary.

Committee #2: Most Truthful Person of the Year—One who always tells you the truth, even if he or she knows it might be painful to hear; one whose words are based on accurate information, not inaccurate; one who doesn't change what he or she says so you'll like him or her better.

Committee #3: Best Teacher of the Year—One who is interested in you as a person; one who knows how to teach so you'll learn; one who challenges you to be the best person you can be.

Committee #4: Best Wilderness Guide of the Year—One who knows the area well and helps you through the dangerous places; one who stays with you all the way; one who cultivates courage in you.

(4) The Holy Spirit has all of the qualities mentioned in question #3. Because He is God, He's the perfect helper; He's perfectly truthful; He's the best teacher available; and He's the best guide for our lives.

Summarize: **The Holy Spirit sounds like someone who is pretty wonderful to have around.**

Expectations

(Needed: Chalkboard and chalk or newsprint and markers)

Explain: **The Holy Spirit is more than our helper, truth giver, teacher, and guide. The Holy Spirit is God Himself who gives us wisdom and shows us things we need to know about Jesus. He also lets us know when we're heading in the wrong direction.**

Write on the board key words from the following statements.

What can we expect the Holy Spirit to do for us in each of the following situations? What can we not expect Him to do?

1. I have to take a hard test in math. (The Holy Spirit will help you stay calm so you can do your best. He will not put answers in your mind if you didn't study.)

2. I'm going to be late getting home and don't know what to tell my parents. (The Holy Spirit can give you the courage to tell the truth. He will not excuse you for lying so you don't get in trouble.)

3. I want to know more about God. (The Holy Spirit will help you understand the Bible when you study it. He will not just put information about God in your mind so you don't have to study.)

4. My friend has the key to his parent's liquor cabinet and wants me to come over and drink with him. (The Holy Spirit will help you say no by reminding you of what's right and giving you the desire to do so. He won't "look the other way" if you disobey.)

5. Someone I like wants me to have sex with him or her. (The Holy Spirit will help you say no by reminding you of what's right and giving you the desire to do so. He won't "look the other way" if you disobey.)

6. My best friend wants me to lie for him so he won't get in trouble. (The Holy Spirit will help you say no by reminding you of what's right and giving you the desire to do so. He won't help you make up lies or "look the other way" if you disobey.)

Say: **Because God is merciful and kind, the Holy Spirit helps us even when we don't have a chance to ask for His help, such as in an emergency. But God does want us to ask for His help when we have the opportunity to do so. When you get involved in situations like the ones we just mentioned, the Holy Spirit is ready and willing to help. So it's important to remember one word.** Write the word *pray* on the board in big letters. **Pray, asking God to guide you, help you, teach you, and show you what's right through the Holy Spirit in you.**

A Look Inside

(Needed: Unshelled peanuts, paper, pencils)

Give each group member an unshelled peanut. Say: **Pretend that this is the first time you've seen a peanut. Someone cracks it open, shows you the nut inside, and tells you that it's good to eat.**

Have group members crack open and eat their peanuts. Then say: **You find that you like it and you want more. The next time you see a peanut, you remember that there is something good inside and you want one.**

Every time you open something and see something good that you like, let it remind you of the Holy Spirit. When you open a present or a door, crack a peanut, peel a banana, or something like that, remember the Holy Spirit and the fact that if you're a Christian, He is living inside of you and is ready to help you.

Even if you're not a Christian, I challenge you to think about the Holy Spirit every time you open something this week. God is more than willing to forgive your sin when you receive Jesus Christ as your Savior. Then He'll send the Holy Spirit to be your counselor, comforter, guide, and teacher.

Distribute paper and pencils. Instruct your group members to draw a picture of something they open often that will remind them of the Holy Spirit from now on.

You may want to take this opportunity to invite kids who are not Christians to stay after the session and talk with you about how to receive Christ as their Savior.

Close the session in prayer, thanking God for the miracle of the indwelling Holy Spirit. Ask God to help you and your group members depend on Him more and more.

THE Spirit OF THE Spirit

1. John 14:15-27 and John 16:13 is full of good news! What statements about the Holy Spirit in John 14:15-27 might help you feel peaceful and confident? Group I = John 14:15-17 / Group II = John 14:18-19 Group III = John 14:20-21 Group IV = John 14:23-25

____

____

2. Jesus uses four words or phrases to describe the Holy Spirit. Here are their definitions. Draw lines connecting the words and phrases to their correct definitions.

COUNSELOR	One who shows what's right in all areas
SPIRIT OF TRUTH	One who shows the way
GUIDE	One who instructs
TEACHER	One who gives aid and comfort

3. Imagine that you're on a committee for a nationwide contest in search of people who qualify to be given one of the following awards. Before you begin your search, you have to define what kind of people you're looking for. Write down the qualifications a person needs in order to receive these awards:

COMMITTEE #1
Most Helpful Person of the Year

COMMITTEE #2
Most Truthful Person of the Year

COMMITTEE #3
Best Teacher of the Year

COMMITTEE #4
Best Wilderness Guide of the Year

4. Would you say the Holy Spirit has the qualifications you listed for question #3? Why or why not?

____

____

Step 2
As you begin to compare Christians to temples of the Holy Spirit, hand out paper and pencils. Ask each person to take a few minutes to draw the "temple" that best reflects his or her character. Most kids probably are much more familiar with churches than actual temples, which is fine. You should help them see that no matter what they look like on the outside, the important thing is that the Holy Spirit is inside. One person might illustrate a chapel in the woods; another might feel more like a big downtown church; another might even perceive himself or herself as a classic European architectural work of genius. Encourage honesty and creative expression. No "residence" is too humble or too big if the Holy Spirit is truly welcomed there.

Step 5
Rather than simply handing each person a peanut, make a game of it. Provide a bag of peanuts for the group and, at a distance, set up open paper bags with the names of group members boldly written across the front. Set a time limit and see who can toss the most peanuts into his or her bag. At the end of the time limit, have everyone pick up his or her bag and count the peanuts inside. (Also have group members pick up all the "strays" scattered across the floor.) Then proceed with Step 5 as written.

Step 1
With a small group, you have the opportunity to start with what group members know about a topic and adapt the session to their specific needs. So as soon as you move from the opening exercises to the introduction of what the session is about, say: **Tell me everything you know about the Holy Spirit. You should suppose I don't know anything about it. Can you help me out?** (One of the first things they should do is correct your choice of pronouns, since the Holy Spirit is a "Him" rather than an "it.") This exercise should not only bring up student questions, but clue you to any misconceptions they have as well.

Step 3
In the intimate setting of a small group, when you get ready to read John 14:15-27, ask one person to assume the role of Jesus and the others to imagine they are His disciples hearing these words for the first time. As the passage is read, the "disciples" should make mental notes of any questions that come to mind. One question is noted within the text, but your group members are likely to have others. After the entire passage has been read, let them express their questions. Many of the questions will be answered as students move on to Repro Resource 6. But if they ask something that will not be covered there, deal with those concerns before passing out copies of the handout.

Step 2
This step concludes with the statement, "The Holy Spirit's presence can bring about great changes in our lives." You might want to take a few minutes at this point to put to work the collective brain power of your many group members. Divide into several teams of four to six people. Ask each team to put together a skit to show a "before-and-after" comparison of a person who has been influenced by the Holy Spirit. Give as few directions as possible so the skits will be varied. Teams might focus on the dramatic differences in wisdom, power, moral concern, relationships, or any number of other changes the Holy Spirit can make. As you continue through the session, you should be able to refer back to several of these skits to emphasize key points you want to make.

Step 3
Another way to get your large group more involved is to let group members act out the "award presentations" listed on Repro Resource 6. Divide into four teams and let each team create an award. The teams should list the qualifications for the award (as instructed on the sheet); but rather than simply read off the awards, they should work them into a presentation speech delivered by one of its members. Then another member could step up to receive the award and give a short acceptance speech. While the two speech-givers are working on what they want to say, the other team members can construct an actual award to present, give it a clever name, and so forth.

Step 1
Before doing anything else, hand each group member an egg. Instruct everyone to hold onto the egg throughout the session. (Just to be safe, you might want to use hard-boiled eggs.) Kids who might be becoming jaded toward Christian truth are the ones who most need to become more sensitive to the leading of the Holy Spirit in their lives. At the end of the session, you can explain that the egg-holding exercise should serve as a reminder of the sensitive nature of the Holy Spirit. We can easily prevent a good relationship with God's Spirit by maintaining improper attitudes: apathy, boredom, self-centeredness, and so forth. If any of the kids' eggs are damaged during the session, your point can be made even stronger.

Step 3
Before you get into a serious discussion about the various roles of the Holy Spirit, let your kids do a roleplay. One person should act as the President of the United States. The others should be his or her staff of advisors (economic, military, foreign affairs, spiritual, and so forth). Have them suppose that the leader of Aruba called the President a "doofus." The President should be offended and desire to declare war on Aruba and attack. His or her staff should offer advice. (Even though the situation is ludicrous, the advisors should act as if the future of the country actually did depend on their decisions.) While you cannot dictate what decision group members reach, it is hoped that they will realize that the offense certainly doesn't warrant the reaction proposed by the President. Then, as you continue the session and talk about the roles of the Holy Spirit, point out that as we learn to respond to the Spirit in our daily lives, He acts as our own inner staff of advisors to help us make the best decisions possible, rather than acting impulsively and getting into unnecessary trouble.

Step 1
If your group members don't have much knowledge of biblical things, the Holy Spirit can be a very difficult concept to deal with. You can't assume that they know about the Trinity, about how God lives in us, or many other basic concepts that most Christians take for granted. Be very conscious of the words you use and the statements you make. In addition, you may want to make a clear distinction between the "fun" parts of this session and the Bible study portion. If you start out by doing tricks and then shift into a discussion of the Holy Spirit, group members might get confused. Also deal with the meaning and implications of the word "spirit" as soon as possible. When they hear the word used, many of these kids may think in terms of Casper the Friendly Ghost or the characters in Dickens' *A Christmas Carol*—neither of which will be helpful as they approach this important biblical truth.

Step 3
When you get ready to read John 14:15-27, take your time in describing the context in which these words were spoken. Explain that Jesus had spent about three years teaching His disciples, healing sick people, performing other miracles, and showing us how we should live. However, He knew He would soon be killed. Ask: **If you had left behind your home, business, and family, and had devoted three whole years of your life to following Jesus around, how do you think you would feel at this point?** Only after group members realize, to some extent, the fears and feelings of the disciples will they be able to understand the importance of Jesus' sending the Holy Spirit to help us out in His absence.

Step 1
If you usually sing as part of your meeting time, focus on songs that deal with the Holy Spirit. Some well-known songs include "We Are One in the Spirit," "Father, I Adore You," "Sweet, Sweet Spirit," "Holy Holy," and so forth. Even if you don't usually sing, it would be appropriate to do so as part of this session. If your group members are up to more of a challenge, have them create a song of their own after the session. Many choruses are only three or four lines with a simple tune. Many musically inclined students should be able to come up with something creative. Or, if you wish, have them write new words to an existing tune.

Step 5
Rather than hoping group members will think of the Holy Spirit by associating His presence with the opening of something in their daily routines, allow time at the end of the session for them to create a more tangible reminder. Provide a variety of craft items (paints, modeling clay, paper, markers, etc.). Ask each person to create something that would symbolize the presence of the Holy Spirit. This may be a bit of a challenge, since the Holy Spirit cannot be seen. Yet most kids should be able to think of something. Try to make yourself available to help anyone who just can't seem to formulate a symbolic concept. When everyone finishes, have each person show what he or she has drawn, sculpted, carved, or built, and explain the symbolism used. Encourage group members to keep their creations in plain sight as reminders during the weeks to come of the Holy Spirit's presence in their lives.

Step 3
Instead of having your group members write down the qualifications for #3 on "The Spirit of the Spirit" (Repro Resource 6), ask them to prepare a team speech. Assign each of four teams one of the awards listed. Instruct each team to discuss the qualifications needed for someone to win that award. Have each team give a name to its winning person. Each team member should then come up with a statement about that person. Explain that each team is to present its "award winner," with each team member playing a part in the process. The teams may choose to present their information as a "cheer," as a choral reading with a leader and response, or as a speech with each person saying a part.

Step 4
Before the session, write the six situations on a separate index cards. Instead of saying the situations, distribute the six cards to six volunteers. Have each volunteer present her situation, adding a few additional comments to further explain the dilemma. Then ask the rest of the group members to come up with some ways the Holy Spirit can help, and some things the Holy Spirit will *not* do, in those situations.

Step 3
When dealing with a subject as complex as the Holy Spirit, try to use a lot of analogies that would help explain His nature and function. A group of mostly guys will probably relate to baseball. So you might say: **When a player is taken out of a game for some reason, or is unable to continue, another person is sent in to play in his place. What are the requirements of who can go in as a substitute?** (He must be on the same team, have the same goals, be willing to work hard to win, and so forth.) **How does this compare to Jesus sending the Holy Spirit?** (When Jesus had completed the job He came to do and could no longer assist His team [all believers] in person, He "sent in" the Holy Spirit who could indwell all believers at once. Jesus and the Holy Spirit had the same nature and purpose, yet different forms and styles of ministry.)

Step 5
With a group of guys, you might want to emphasize that in addition to the wisdom skills provided by the Holy Spirit (counseling, guiding, teaching, and leading into truth), He also provides power. Ask: **What are some of the things guys do to try to show how manly or macho they are?** (Take foolish dares; refuse to cry, no matter how much they are hurt; put down other people—especially women; etc.) These are all nonproductive wastes of energy. In reality, such behaviors reveal weaknesses rather than prove strengths. Explain that since we possess the Spirit of God, we don't need to act tough. To become truly strong, we must learn to tap into the power we have at our disposal. Then we will truly be (or at least become) strong. Only by the leading of God's Spirit will we ever be able to become tough enough to withstand intense pressure while remaining sensitive to the needs and feelings of others. That's a winning combination for success in life that too few guys will ever discover.

Step 2
Bring in several balloons and two sets of long underwear. Divide into two teams. Each team should choose one person to wear the long johns over his or her clothes. At your signal, everyone else should blow up balloons, tie the ends, and stuff the balloons into the long underwear. After four or five minutes, you should signal again for everyone to stop. Count the balloons accumulated by each team (perhaps by popping one at a time with a straight pin, through the long underwear) and declare a winner. Refer to the unusual appearance of the volunteers as they were stuffed with balloons as you explain that this may be the image some people have when they hear references to "God living in their hearts" or "being temples of the Holy Spirit." It seems unnatural, and indeed, it is. It's supernatural. But allowing the Holy Spirit to be part of one's life is a simple matter of willing obedience—and the results are better than we might expect.

Step 5
Divide into teams for a relay race. You'll need a two-liter bottle of cola for each team. The bottles should be set at the opposite end of the room from where the teams are lined up. The first person on the team should run to the bottle and remove the cap. The next several team members should drink the cola, with each person chugging as much as possible in one trip. (If group members don't want to drink after each other, provide cups for them.) When all the cola is gone, the next person in line is responsible for filling up the bottle with water. (Have some on hand, or let the players run to a nearby sink or fountain.) When the bottle has been filled with water, the next person in line should put the cap back on. Afterward, explain how this activity symbolizes God's Spirit coming into a person's life. The old ways, sinful and dirty, can be replaced with new, godly ways. The transition is not instantaneous in experience—it's something we should work on throughout our lives.

Step 2
Preview and show a video clip of a film in which the plot revolves around a main character having something inside of him or her. Then have group members brainstorm other examples they can think of. A few to get them started are *Rosemary's Baby* (the child of the devil), the *Alien* series (evil space aliens), *The Hidden* (another evil space alien), *Sybil* (multiple personalities), *Star Wars* (the "force"), *The Terminator* (a cyborg underneath human-looking skin) and, of course, *Peter Pan* (if you count the crocodile that swallowed the ticking clock as a main character). It seems that Hollywood is somewhat fascinated with this theme. But movie makers have yet to come up with anything as powerful or exciting as the Holy Spirit, who resides within each person who puts his or her faith in Jesus.

Step 3
To follow up your discussion of the Holy Spirit, have your group members create an episode of "In Search Of" or some related sensationalistic investigative-reporting TV show. Many kids have probably seen reports on topics such as the Loch Ness monster, Bigfoot, UFOs, or other strange phenomena. But their topic now should be: "In search of . . . the Holy Spirit. No one has ever seen Him, yet thousands of people insist He exists." Let group members determine how they might go about proving the existence of the Holy Spirit (through interviews, observations of changed lives, etc.). Videotape their efforts so that later they can take a look at how well they did.

Step 1
Performing a series of tricks is an effective opener, yet can be time consuming. As an alternative, you might want to consider having a number of packages sitting on the table as students arrive. When the meeting begins, let a few volunteers each choose one. Explain that some of the packages might have good stuff inside, some might have bad stuff, and some might be empty. (A few of your packages should appear very fancy—shiny paper, ribbons, bows, the works. A few should be wrapped in old newspapers or simply placed in brown paper bags. Others should be in between. Take great care in seeing that the good prizes, bogus prizes, and empty packages are divided among all of the kinds of wrapping so that no patterns can be detected.) Let all of the volunteers open their packages at once and show what they got, if anything. Ask a few of them why they chose the package they did. Explain that this session will deal with the Holy Spirit. Point out that people are like these packages—if you judge only from outward appearances, you aren't usually able to tell who does or doesn't have God's Spirit dwelling within him or her.

Step 3
You can save additional time by simply reading and discussing John 14:15-27 as a group, rather than using Repro Resource 6. If it looks as if you still won't have time to finish, you can select just one of the six examples from Step 4. (The key is to keep up the pace as you go through the steps on the handout. The rest of the session isn't very time consuming.)

Step 2
If your teens are unfamiliar with the term "Holy Spirit," consider comparing Him to the following:
• a tutor
• a tour guide at a museum
• a stagehand who throws the spotlight on the star (Jesus)
• a paramedic who comes to help or rescue someone
• a psychologist
• a bodyguard.

Step 5
If you cannot easily obtain shelled peanuts for this activity, a couple of bags of peanut M & Ms will serve equally well.

Step 3
Perhaps no wish is as strong or as common among junior highers as the desire to have a driver's license. Ask: **What things will you be able to do when you get a driver's license that you can't do now? Which of the things that you've mentioned do you plan to do?** Encourage group members to be as specific as possible in their responses. Don't let them get by with "I'll get out of the house!" Press them to find out exactly where they'd like to go and what they'd like to do. Then, as you introduce the topic of the Holy Spirit, try to explain that there are things we want to be able to do as human beings that we can never accomplish without the help of God's Spirit (such as become good, forgive parents, like ourselves for who we are, overcome strong temptations, reach our maximum potential, etc.). Receiving God's Holy Spirit in our lives provides us with the freedom to get beyond where we have become "stuck"—much like a driver's license provides the freedom to get out of our parents' house.

Step 5
In addition to sending your junior highers home to find their own reminders of the Holy Spirit, give them a headstart as well. Hand out boxes of Cracker Jack to everyone. Perhaps your group members are a little too old to look forward to the prize in the box, but they will probably remember the excitement they felt as younger kids. Point out that the Holy Spirit in the life of a Christian is a truly valuable prize—not like a plastic figure or washable tattoo. But the concept is the same. We have something inside us that we (and others) can get excited about if we know enough to look for it.

Step 2
Students willing to dig a little deeper than most might enjoy seeing exactly how important the tabernacle (and later the temple) was to God's people. This was no pup tent pitched in haste as the people moved through the wilderness. If you have good reference books with pictures and easy-to-understand articles, try to have them on hand for one group to examine. Let another group skim through Exodus 25–31; 35–40. The members of this group will see the incredible detail and some of the symbolism that went into planning the tabernacle and its furnishings. A third group can skim through I Kings 5–8 and see the similar attention given to Solomon's temple. After this kind of examination, it should mean a bit more when group members hear that *they* are temples of the Holy Spirit.

Step 3
We may tend to use the term "Holy Spirit" without too much thought. But it can be helpful for willing students to do a word study to find out more about what "holy" and "spirit" mean, as well as to discover more about the Holy Spirit Himself. You might also want to deal with the theological concept of the Trinity, since the session doesn't do so. Provide Bible dictionaries and concordances. First, come to some agreement on good working definitions for the terms, and then go to the concordances for other biblical examples and information. (You may wish to single out a few key verses ahead of time for students to explore, or you might want to devote an entire additional meeting to this option.)

Date Used:

Approx. Time

Step 1: Tricked! ______
o Small Group
o Heard It All Before
o Little Bible Background
o Fellowship & Worship
o Short Meeting Time
Things needed:

Step 2: An Awesome Fact ______
o Extra Action
o Large Group
o Extra Fun
o Media
o Urban
o Extra Challenge
Things needed:

Step 3: Meet the Holy Spirit ______
o Small Group
o Large Group
o Heard It All Before
o Little Bible Background
o Mostly Girls
o Mostly Guys
o Media
o Short Meeting Time
o Combined Junior High/High School
o Extra Challenge
Things needed:

Step 4: Expectations ______
o Mostly Girls
Things needed:

Step 5: A Look Inside ______
o Extra Action
o Fellowship & Worship
o Mostly Guys
o Extra Fun
o Urban
o Combined Junior High/High School
Things needed:

SESSION 5

How Do I "Walk" with God?

YOUR GOALS FOR THIS SESSION:

Choose one or more

- [ ] To help kids recognize the importance of having someone to help them through life's everyday problems.
- [ ] To help kids understand how the Holy Spirit can help us with our everyday problems.
- [ ] To help kids commit to "walking in the Spirit."
- [ ] Other ____________________

Your Bible Base:

II Corinthians 1:19-22
Galatians 5:16-26

Making It Through

(Needed: Large boxes, newspapers, chairs, rolls of tape, large bandanas or scarves, prizes [optional])

Have group members form two teams. Assign each team one half of the room. Instruct each team to use whatever objects are available in the room—including shoes, jackets, and the supplies you've provided—to make an obstacle course. [NOTE: Make sure you identify the things in the room you do *not* want used.]

After the teams have completed their courses, the members of Team A (one at a time) will run through Team B's course as quickly as they can without moving or knocking over any of the obstacles. However, the members of Team B may handicap members of Team A by blindfolding them, putting their arms in slings, or anything else (within the realm of safety) that will make it more difficult to get through the course.

After all the members of Team A have run Team B's course, the members of Team B will run Team A's course. Team A will then get to "handicap" the members of Team B.

After both teams have finished running the courses, you may want to award prizes for the most creative or difficult obstacle course.

Then ask: **Have you had a day recently that seemed like an obstacle course? If so, what were some of the obstacles you faced?** (Group members might mention things like a pop quiz, disagreement with parents, needing money for something but not having it, etc.)

How did you feel at the end of your "obstacle course" day? (Depressed, disgusted, angry, tired, etc.)

Say: **When we face this kind of day, we have two choices. We can try to make it through alone, or we can get some help. Let's talk about the kinds of help that are available to us.**

STEP 2

When You Need a Friend

(Needed: Cut-apart copies of Repro Resource 7)

Before the session, you'll need to cut apart the cards on "Walk with Me" (Repro Resource 7). Distribute the cards to eight volunteers. (If your group is small, you can give more than one card to each volunteer.) One at a time, have the volunteers read aloud their cards (in numerical order 1-8).

After each card has been read, have your group members explain how they might react to that situation. Then have group members suggest how their responses might be different if someone else were facing the situation with them.

For instance, for #4, a group member's reaction might be to say a few choice words to the cafeteria workers and then complain bitterly about the food at the lunch table. However, if another person were facing the situation too, the two of them might joke about it and vent their frustrations through laughter.

Afterward, ask: **Have you ever gone through a tough experience alone that would have been easier to deal with if you'd some help? Explain.**

Has someone ever helped you get through a tough time? Explain. Encourage responses from several group members.

Summarize: **Having someone around who is truly helpful can save us energy, time, stress, and can sometimes even spare us from deep sorrow or distress.**

STEP 3

The One Who Walks with Us

(Needed: Bibles, dictionary)

Say: **It's great to have good friends or loving family members to help us along the way. But sometimes, we need more**

help than they can give. We need the help of Almighty God. And His help can come through the Holy Spirit, who, as we've discussed, lives in each Christian. The Holy Spirit is here to walk through each day with us. Let's find out what that means.

Have volunteers take turns reading aloud Galatians 5:16-26. Then ask: **What instructions are we given in verses 16 and 25?** (To live by the Spirit.)

What do you think it means to "live by the Spirit?" If group members don't mention it, point out that the passage defines it further as not gratifying "the desires of the sinful nature" (vs. 16) and keeping "in step with the Spirit" (vs. 25). Some might also say that it means to obey what the Holy Spirit says to do, follow His guidance, and do what is right.

According to this passage in Galatians, what can happen if we don't live by the Spirit? Some acts of the sinful nature are listed in verses 19-21. Have each group member read and then define in their own words one of the acts of the sinful nature. Allow group members to use a dictionary if they need help.

After each word is defined, have group members give a "thumbs-up" sign if the act is something that kids today might be tempted to participate in.

You may want to summarize the passage by reading the following definitions from the Living Bible: "impure thoughts, eagerness for lustful pleasure, idolatry, spiritism (that is, encouraging the activity of demons), hatred and fighting, jealousy and anger, constant effort to get the best for yourself, complaints and criticisms, the feeling that everyone else is wrong except those in your own little group—and there will be wrong doctrine, envy, murder, drunkenness, wild parties, and all that sort of thing."

Say: **This list of sin seems to go on and on. It's amazing that so much evil can result from disobeying God.** Point out that since most of these activities are still tempting for us today, we *need* to walk in the Holy Spirit.

What are the benefits of living by the Spirit? (Love, joy, peace, patience, kindness, goodness, faithfulness, gentleness, and self-control [vss. 22, 23].)

Encourage group members to give specific examples of each of the fruit of the Spirit. After each example is given, have group members give a "thumbs-up" sign if they would like to experience that fruit in their own lives or if they're already experiencing it.

Giant Steps

(Needed: Copies of Repro Resource 8, pennies or paper clips, prizes [optional])

Distribute a copy of "Backward or Forward" (Repro Resource 8) and a paper clip or penny to each group member.

Explain: **On your sheet, you have two lists—a list of the acts of the sinful nature and a list of the fruit of the Spirit. You also have a game board. Put your penny/paper clip on the "Start" square.**

I'm going to read several situations. After I read each one, you'll decide whether it's an act of the sinful nature or a fruit of the Spirit. Then you'll look at the appropriate list on your sheet and decide which act of the sinful nature or fruit of the Spirit is being described. The first person to stand and give the correct answer gets to move his or her playing piece to the next square. If you identify an act of the sinful nature, you'll move backward. If you identify a fruit of the Spirit, you'll move forward. The first person to reach either end square is the winner.

You may want to award a prize to the winner. If no one reaches one of the end squares before you run out of situations, award the prize to the person who is closest to one of the end squares. Point out that there may be more than one correct answer for each situation.

The situations are as follows:

(1) You watch an X-rated video at a friend's house. (Act of the sinful nature—sexual immorality, impurity, or debauchery.)

(2) You are so anxious to get a car that you agree to sell marijuana to make some money. (Act of the sinful nature—idolatry or selfish ambition.)

(3) You invite a kid of another race who's new at school to eat lunch with you. (Fruit of the Spirit—love, kindness, or goodness.)

(4) You start going to meetings where kids say they can help you gain magic powers. (Act of the sinful nature—witchcraft.)

(5) When one of your friends tells someone else a secret you told him or her in confidence, you plan ways to get even with him or her. (Act of the sinful nature—hatred, discord, or fits of rage.)

(6) Instead of blowing up at your kid brother when he

comes into your room for the fifth time and asks you to play with him, you keep your cool and promise to do so after dinner. (Fruit of the Spirit—patience, love, kindness, goodness.)

(7) Because you're angry with your parents for grounding you, you keep complaining about little things your family members do. (Act of the sinful nature—hatred, discord, or fits of rage.)

(8) You have to give a speech in assembly and you're scared, but you pray and sense a calmness growing inside. (Fruit of the Spirit—peace.)

(9) You blew up and cussed out your sister because she took the car after your dad said you could have it this evening. (Act of the sinful nature—hatred, discord, or fits of rage.)

(10) You were very angry because your sister took the car after your dad said you could have it, but you prayed to keep control and took a long walk to calm down. (Fruit of the Spirit—patience or self-control.)

(11) You wish you were dating your best friend's boyfriend or girlfriend. (Act of the sinful nature—envy or jealousy.)

(12) You and another kid at school are competing for the same job. You lie to your potential employer by making up a terrible lie about your competitor. (Act of the sinful nature—selfish ambition.)

(13) You obey God even though you are cruelly made fun of for it by kids at school. (Fruit of the Spirit—love or faithfulness.)

After you've declared a winner, go through the "acts of the sinful nature" situations again. Have your group members suggest ways they could "walk in the Spirit" in each situation, rather than giving in to the sinful nature.

Use the following ideas to supplement group members' responses.

(1) Pray for courage to say no to the X-rated video and for creativity in coming up with a better idea.

(2) Pray about your desire for the car and for the patience to wait for what God wants you to do.

(4) Heed God's Word and run fast in the other direction when black magic or witchcraft is mentioned.

(5) Let the person know how angry you are, but that you're also asking God to help you forgive him or her.

(7) Obey your parents; pray for self-control in handling your anger.

(9) Apologize to your sister; ask God's forgiveness.

(11) Ask God to forgive you for envying your friend and to give you the patience to wait for the person He may have for you.

(12) Tell your potential employer you lied. Apologize to your competitor, if wise Christians counsel you to do so. Ask God to forgive you for lying and for your selfish ambition.

Ask: **Are you taking steps backward or forward in your**

walk with God? If you're having sex with someone, losing your temper, causing problems at home, you know the answer.

If you aren't a Christian, you need to turn to God. If you are a Christian, you need to let the Holy Spirit change you by obeying Him.

Spend time with God regularly—in the Bible and in prayer. Try listening to Christian music. As a result of being with God, you'll begin to love God. Then you'll want to walk with Him. You might ask group members to name other suggestions for ways to "walk with God."

Count on It

(Needed: Bibles, chalkboard and chalk or newsprint and markers)

Have your group members quickly name five things they can count on about school. (For example: I can count on having homework; getting in trouble if I disobey the rules; having tests; getting a report card; being bored; etc.)

Then have someone read aloud II Corinthians 1:19-22. As a group, list five things from the passage God says we can count on. Summarize the answers on the board as follows.

1. God means what He says.
2. God does what He promises.
3. God is faithful.
4. God helps us become strong.
5. God has given us His Spirit.

Point out that there are five points, one for each finger. As time permits, have group members memorize the five points and recite them to the person sitting next to them.

Summarize: **If we choose to walk in the Spirit, we can count on the fact that He will always be our "inside Friend." He'll keep His promises to help with our decisions and to provide courage when we need it. All we have to do is ask.**

Close the session in prayer, thanking God for giving us His Holy Spirit and asking for His help in "walking in the Spirit."

Walk with Me

1. At breakfast you spill grape juice on the jacket you have to wear for a school choir concert today.

2. Even though you're running late for school, your dad won't let you take the car.

3. Because you're late for school, you miss a quiz and have to make it up after school. That means you can't go horseback riding with your friend.

4. For lunch in the cafeteria, all they have are wiener roll-ups. You hate wiener roll-ups. You have a few choice words you'd like to say to the cook.

5. When you get home from school, your mom reminds you that you have to rake leaves. You moan and groan. She doesn't seem to care about the bad day you had.

6. While you're raking leaves, the pesky kid next door comes over to watch—and ask a hundred questions. You want to tell him to get lost.

7. Your mom serves liver for dinner. You hate liver and she knows it.

8. After dinner you go to your room to sulk. Just to annoy everyone, you blast your stereo. Life is one big pain.

BACKWARD OR FORWARD

SINFUL NATURE

SEXUAL IMMORALITY
Impurity
Debauchery
IDOLATRY
Witchcraft
Hatred
Discord
Jealousy
Fits of rage
Selfish ambition
Dissensions
Factions
Envy
Drunkenness
Orgies

FRUIT OF THE SPIRIT

Love
Joy
PEACE
Patience
Kindness
Goodness
FAITHFULNESS
Gentleness
Self-control

Step 3
A good way to demonstrate the challenge to "keep in step with the Spirit" is to have a three-legged race. Have group members pair up, stand side-by-side, and tie their inside legs together. If you still have your obstacle course set up, perhaps you can adapt it for this relay. Otherwise, just set up a start and finish line in a large open area. When the race is over, have the winners share the secret of their success; then let the others discuss some of the difficulties they faced in trying to keep in step with their partners. Move from this into some of the obvious spiritual applications for keeping in step with the Holy Spirit.

Step 4
The "Backward or Forward" game in Repro Resource 8 can easily be adapted into a more active exercise. Let kids serve as their own game pieces, standing shoulder to shoulder in the center of the room. You can play the game the same way, or you might choose to provide people with pens and paper to write down their answers to each question. Allow all those who answer correctly to move, rather than limiting the opportunity to the first person to raise his or her hand.

Step 1
A small group split in half may not provide enough people to construct two challenging obstacle courses; so you might want to set one up yourself, before the meeting. Or perhaps you know of a good obstacle course in a park or playground in your area. If so, it may take less time to pile your group members into a car and go to where the obstacles are than to try to construct a course of your own.

Step 2
If performed as directed, Repro Resource 7 requires ten people. It can be adapted to your group, of course, but here's another alternative. After you deal with the topic of physical, tangible obstacles (in Step 1), ask kids to brainstorm the other kinds of obstacles they face. They should consider all areas of their lives—home and family, school, work, church, and so forth. List all of the obstacles on the board as they are named, without making comments or observations on them. Then, after you have a good list, go through it one obstacle at a time and let each person express how much of a problem it is in his or her life. (An easy way to do this is to have group members rate each item on a 1 to 10 priority scale [with 10 being highest], holding up the appropriate number of fingers to indicate their answers.) Not only will group members be able to quickly see how many others share their personal concerns, but you will be able to determine which are the major problem areas. You can then plan future sessions to deal with the specific needs of your group.

Step 1
Divide into teams of four or five. Except for the members of one team, have everyone stand in the center of the room. Members of the designated team must wear some kind of hat. Set a time limit. The object of the game is to see how many times team members can run from one end of the room to the other without having their hats pulled off. The runners may not hold onto their hats; the people in the center may not hold or impede the runners. A point is scored for each time someone makes it all the way across. (A runner may score as many points as possible within the time period.) When time is up, the team's points are totaled. The team then switches places with a team in the center. Continue until all the teams have served as runners; then declare the winners.

Step 2
A large group may need more involvement than is provided by Repro Resource 7. If that's the case with your group, try the following activity. Have everyone stand in the center of the room. You will name a category. Group members should then divide into the groups you specify for that category. For example, you might say: **The category is age. Find everyone else in the room who is your age.** You might want to make a contest of this by awarding points to the people in the first group to form, and taking away points from the people in the last group to form. Here are some other categories to use:
- Month of birth
- Day of birth
- School attended
- Street address (even numbers vs. odd)
- Hair color
- Amount of money in pockets, wallet, or purse (over $5 vs. under $5)

Afterward, point out that other people probably share a lot of our problems, anxieties, and fears. Perhaps we just need to look a bit harder when we think we're alone in our sufferings.

OPTIONS

SESSION FIVE

Step 2
Instead of using Repro Resource 7, focus more on the follow-up to the obstacle course activity. Distribute paper and pencils. Instruct group members to write "Obstacles, Obstacles, Obstacles" down the left side of their papers. Then have them think of as many obstacles in their lives as possible that begin with those letters. (Allow them to use adjectives if they wish. For instance, if they would like to write "parents" but don't have a "P," they can write "ornery parents.") When group members finish, try to get them talking about the most common and most annoying obstacles they've listed. Then discuss how things might be different if they had a constant companion who could help them through difficult situations.

Step 3
Before looking at Galatians 5:16-26, have group members do a roleplay. Before the session, write out the sins of the sinful nature listed in verses 19-21 on separate slips of paper (with definitions, if needed). Give one to each group member and ask him or her to assume that characteristic. Have one other volunteer roleplay an average high school student going to a party. The people assuming the sinful characteristics should greet him or her, one or two at a time, and be as creative as possible in demonstrating their "nature." The "innocent" volunteer should wander from person to person, listening to their comments and deciding whether or not to do the things they suggest. Afterward, ask: **Did any of these people remind you of real people you know? How would you like to be in a situation like this one? How can we keep from finding ourselves in such circumstances?** In discussing the Galatians passage, help group members see that this was the kind of thing Paul was trying to warn us about. If we don't allow God's Spirit to provide us with positive "fruit," we won't just be *exposed* to sins like those in the skit—we will be the ones *doing* them.

Step 3
Long-time Christians may be familiar with terms like "walking in the Spirit" and "keeping in step with the Spirit," but other people might not be. These aren't exactly the easiest things to understand for someone who is trying to absorb these truths for the first time. One thing that might be helpful would be to first speak in terms of Jesus and His disciples. Say: **When Jesus was on earth, He walked along the shores of Galilee and taught His followers important things. They learned from Him, laughed with Him, prayed with Him, and did everything together. When Jesus left, they pretty much fell apart for a while. But Jesus had promised to send them the Holy Spirit. After the Spirit came to live inside the followers of Jesus, all of those people became dynamic individuals even though the earthly Jesus was no longer there. The same is true today. The Spirit of God lives inside all Christians. We are able to talk to Him, walk with Him, and communicate with a real, live person. Sure, it's a little more difficult to learn to interact with an invisible, intangible Spirit, but it becomes easier with practice.**

Step 5
Second Corinthians 1:19-22 is not an easy passage to understand at first reading—or second, or third. If your kids aren't used to biblical language or concepts, you might want to explain just the five things to remember and where they came from. Also, don't expect your group members to make their own applications as more experienced churchgoers might. Even though they can memorize the five things as instructed, it would probably be very helpful for you to talk them through some specific examples of each one. As good as these promises are, they won't mean much if kids aren't able to relate them to real life.

Step 2
Rather than moving through Repro Resource 7 as just another step in the session, take a few minutes to build fellowship. One at a time, ask group members to express the current obstacles in their lives. Be patient during this time. If kids aren't used to opening up about the things that bother them, they may be reluctant at first. Perhaps you could list several things from your own life to get everyone started. As other individuals begin to share, make a master list of the obstacles of your group. During the next week, make copies to hand out to everyone the next time you meet. Ask group members to commit to pray for each other during the next few weeks (beginning today). Their obstacles will be more easily overcome when they are aware that several other people are relating to the things they are experiencing.

Step 5
After you read II Corinthians 1:19-22 and have group members memorize the five things they can count on God doing for them, let them go one step farther. Provide paper and pens and ask them to complete sentences based on each of the things they've memorized. For example:
- **Because God means what He says, I will . . .**
- **Because God does what He promises, I . . .**
- **Because God is faithful, I can count on Him to . . .**
- **Because God helps me become strong, I am able to . . .**
- **Because God has given me His Spirit, I . . .**

This exercise helps group members create some personal applications for the things they've learned. If some kids are willing, let them share some of the things they've written; but don't put pressure on anyone. It's enough for them to make personal commitments based on what they've learned.

Step 2

You'll need lunch bags and markers for this activity. Have your group members make very simple paper-bag puppets. The puppets are made by turning the flat bag upside down and drawing a mouth at the fold created by the bottom. Operate the puppet by inserting one hand into the bag and grasping the fold, pressing the fingers toward the palm and/or opening them to make the mouth move. After the puppets are made, have group members form teams of two to four. Distribute a copy of "Walk with Me" (Repro Resource 7) to each team. Instruct the teams to use their puppets to respond to the obstacles in that day. Give the teams a few minutes to work; then have them present their puppet shows. Afterward, discuss the questions at the end of the step

Step 5

As you discuss the five things group members can count on about God, ask: **How does knowing these things affect how you feel about God? Which of these things best helps you understand that God is a part of your life and not just a powerful Spirit removed from everyday situations?**

Step 1

With a mostly masculine group, you might want to be a lot more aggressive with the obstacle course activity. It may even be difficult to construct something within the room that would be sufficiently challenging for them. If so, consider adding the element of physical exercise along the way. ("Crawl through the empty box and then do twenty-five sit-ups. Go through the door backward and then do a dozen pull-ups on the overhead beam. Limbo under the table and then do ten push-ups.") As each person runs the obstacle course, you might let the others attempt to impede his progress by throwing balls at him, placing new obstacles in his path, or whatever. Better yet, let your guys come up with their own challenges and see what happens.

Step 3

When you get to Galatians 5:19-21, take your time discussing the significance of the sins listed there. Most of the things in the list are "guy sins"—things that are especially indicative of or tempting to teenage guys. Don't generalize these things too quickly and move on to the fruit of the Spirit. In fact, you might want to go through the list one at a time and let group members come up with all of the specific instances of that problem that they've encountered during the previous week. Before doing so, however, make sure that they know you will not be overly shocked by anything they say, and that whatever they mention will be held in confidence. Only when they are allowed to deal more deeply with the specifics of their own sinful natures will the fruit of the Spirit seem more like a valid answer for them.

Step 2

Before you begin this step, arrange chairs in a circle. Have everyone sit in the chairs except for one person, who will stand in the center. There should be an empty chair in the circle. The goal of the person in the center is to sit down. However, the rest of the seated people will try to make sure that he doesn't have that opportunity. As the center person moves toward the open seat, the others should shift seats and fill in the space. Of course, one seat is always open. When the center person is finally able to sit in the open chair, he designates someone else to go to the center. After you play for a while, point out how frustrating it is when some of our closest friends become obstacles for us. Then move into Repro Resource 7 and see how people can help us overcome our obstacles, rather than making them worse.

Step 3

Have group members arrange their chairs in a circle. As you go through the list of the acts of the sinful nature in Galatians 5:19-21, read one sin at a time. Ask group members to move one chair to either the right or left (your discretion) for every time today (or this week) they've either committed that sin or come into contact with it. (They need not say which.) Of course, soon people will begin to pile up in certain chairs while other chairs remain empty, but that's OK. Just go to the next one on the list and do the same thing. For several of the sins listed, you might want to include examples as well as definitions of the terms used. After you go through the list of sins, have group members return to their original chairs. Then do the same thing for the list of characteristics of the fruit of the Spirit (vss. 22, 23).

Step 3
Most video stores contain "blooper" videos of various sports. These make very entertaining (and enlightening) examples of what happens when people get "out of step" in some kind of sport. The application then becomes apparent as to what happens to us on a spiritual level when we get out of step with the Holy Spirit in our lives. Sometimes it's not a pretty sight. [NOTE: If the video you choose is labeled "For private use only," it is not intended to be shown in a group setting. Many publishers don't mind as long as you aren't charging admission to see it, but it is still appropriate for you to write them for permission to use specified portions in your group.]

Step 4
Instead of doing Repro Resource 8, provide several magazines for your group members to go through. After you've discussed the acts of the sinful nature in Galatians 5:19-21, ask group members to examine the ads for suggestions of any of these characteristics. It shouldn't be too hard to find examples of lust, selfish ambition, or envy. And with a little effort, you should be able to find several others on the list as well. In several secular magazines aimed at teens, some of the ads can be quite graphic. And be forewarned—some of these ads occasionally include partial nudity (bare breasts or buttocks), so you might want to look through the magazines first to avoid any surprises.

Step 1
After your group members run the obstacle course, skip to Step 3 and discuss the Galatians 5 list of sins. Explain that these things are obstacles in our lives. Ask: **Which of the things on this list are the hardest things for you to deal with? Do you think some are worse than others?** (Perhaps, but sin is sin as far as God is concerned.) **How do you think you can get over or around these obstacles?** Let the discussion lead to the rest of the passage, in which the fruit of the Spirit is introduced. Then spend the rest of the time discussing these questions: **What has God done to help us get around all of these obstacles? Based on what He has done, what can we do to keep from being tripped up by any of these things?**

Step 2
Another option is to eliminate the opening obstacle course, since it can be time consuming. Also skip Repro Resource 7, since it is a follow-up exercise. Begin with the questions at the end of Step 2 and move right into Step 3. Depending on the time you have remaining, Step 4 can be optional. (Rather than playing the game on Repro Resource 8, you may want to simply select a couple of examples to show kids specifically what kinds of things they might expect and how they can choose to respond.) Then conclude with Step 5 as written.

Step 3
After you've discussed the fruit of the Spirit, ask your group members to consider (a) how they can be applied to the city in general, and (b) what type of urban people need the fruit being applied most. For example, love may be needed by runaways and prostitutes, while kindness may be needed by those who use their riches to oppress, rather than to bless.

Step 4
Here are some urban-centered scenarios you might use for the activity:
(1) You take a gun or knife to school for protection. (Act of the sinful nature—hatred, fits of rage, factions.)
(2) You volunteer for a soup kitchen after school. (Fruit of the Spirit—kindness.)
(3) You decide to get out of an abusive relationship before things get further out of hand. (Fruit of the Spirit—peace, self-control.)
(4) You are sixteen and involved in a sexual relationship with a person who is thirty-four years old. (Act of the sinful nature—sexual immorality, impurity, discord, selfish ambition.)

Step 2
If you have a group of mostly junior highers, you might want to replace Repro Resource 7 with a discussion of the following questions: **What are some obstacles that junior highers face that no one else does? What things do you go through that other people just don't seem to understand?** Your group members may not have thought much about this, but have them spend some time coming up with the things that are particularly challenging for them: going through puberty; having a desire to get out and get around, but not being able to drive; being treated like kids half of the time and adults the other half; too much parental control; etc. After you help group members zero in on some specific things, the rest of the session may seem more applicable to them.

Step 3
When you get to the Galatians 5 list of acts of the sinful nature, junior highers may need considerable more explanation of the definitions of some of the terms. But they might also need a little incentive to differentiate one from the rest. One way to hold their attention is to give them a list of the words (as on Repro Resource 8). Then read one definition at a time from a dictionary. Let kids try to match each definition you read with the appropriate term on their lists. This is a relatively quick way to cover all of the definitions you need to review with your junior highers.

Step 4
At the end of this step are a number of ideas to supplement group members' previous responses. For an extra challenge, have your students think of an appropriate Bible verse or passage that will support each of the ideas. In cases where they cannot think of one, have them use a concordance to find one. It's one thing to "Pray for courage and say no to the X-rated video"; but it can be even more assuring to reaffirm the truth of Philippians 4:13: "I can do everything through him who gives me strength." And when the kids generate their own biblical support, they are likely to remember the passages longer than they would if you supply them.

Step 5
When you read II Corinthians 1:19-22, explain that this was a message Paul was trying to communicate to the Corinthian church in the first century. However, it may be a bit hard to understand for teenagers in the twentieth century. Challenge group members to paraphrase Paul's message as they might explain it to their friends. This can be done either individually or in small groups.

Date Used:

Approx. Time

Step 1: Making It Through _____
o Small Group
o Large Group
o Mostly Guys
o Short Meeting Time
Things needed:

Step 2: When You Need a Friend _____
o Small Group
o Large Group
o Heard It All Before
o Fellowship & Worship
o Mostly Girls
o Extra Fun
o Short Meeting Time
o Combined Junior High/High School
Things needed:

Step 3: The One Who Walks with Us _____
o Extra Action
o Heard It All Before
o Little Bible Background
o Mostly Guys
o Extra Fun
o Media
o Urban
o Combined Junior High/High School
Things needed:

Step 4: Giant Steps _____
o Extra Action
o Media
o Urban
o Extra Challenge
Things needed:

Step 5: Count on It _____
o Little Bible Background
o Fellowship & Worship
o Mostly Girls
o Extra Challenge
Things needed:

Custom Curriculum Critique

Please take a moment to fill out this evaluation form, rip it out, fold it, tape it, and send it back to us. This will help us continue to customize products for you. Thanks!

1. Overall, please give this *Custom Curriculum* course (*Is Anybody There?*) a grade in terms of how well it worked for you. (A=excellent; B=above average; C=average; D=below average; F=failure) Circle one.

   A B C D F

2. Now assign a grade to each part of this curriculum that you used.

a. Upfront article	A	B	C	D	F	Didn't use
b. Publicity/Clip art	A	B	C	D	F	Didn't use
c. Repro Resource Sheets	A	B	C	D	F	Didn't use
d. Session 1	A	B	C	D	F	Didn't use
e. Session 2	A	B	C	D	F	Didn't use
f. Session 3	A	B	C	D	F	Didn't use
g. Session 4	A	B	C	D	F	Didn't use
h. Session 5	A	B	C	D	F	Didn't use

3. How helpful were the options?
   ❏ Very helpful ❏ Not too helpful
   ❏ Somewhat helpful ❏ Not at all helpful

4. Rate the amount of options:
   ❏ Too many
   ❏ About the right amount
   ❏ Too few

5. Tell us how often you used each type of option (4=Always; 3=Sometimes; 2=Seldom; 1=Never)

	4	3	2	1
Extra Action	❏	❏	❏	❏
Combined Jr. High/High School	❏	❏	❏	❏
Urban	❏	❏	❏	❏
Small Group	❏	❏	❏	❏
Large Group	❏	❏	❏	❏
Extra Fun	❏	❏	❏	❏
Heard It All Before	❏	❏	❏	❏
Little Bible Background	❏	❏	❏	❏
Short Meeting Time	❏	❏	❏	❏
Fellowship and Worship	❏	❏	❏	❏
Mostly Guys	❏	❏	❏	❏
Mostly Girls	❏	❏	❏	❏
Media	❏	❏	❏	❏
Extra Challenge (High School only)	❏	❏	❏	❏
Sixth Grade (Jr. High only)	❏	❏	❏	❏

(tape here)

BUSINESS REPLY MAIL
FIRST CLASS MAIL PERMIT NO 1 ELGIN IL

POSTAGE WILL BE PAID BY ADDRESSEE

Attn: Youth Department
David C Cook Publishing Co
850 N GROVE AVE
ELGIN IL 60120-9980

NO POSTAGE NECESSARY IF MAILED IN THE UNITED STATES

6. What did you like best about this course?

7. What suggestions do you have for improving *Custom Curriculum*?

8. Other topics you'd like to see covered in this series:

9. Are you?
   ❑ Full time paid youthworker
   ❑ Part time paid youthworker
   ❑ Volunteer youthworker

10. When did you use *Custom Curriculum*?
    ❑ Sunday School ❑ Small Group
    ❑ Youth Group ❑ Retreat
    ❑ Other ____________________

11. What grades did you use it with? ____________

12. How many kids used the curriculum in an average week? ________

13. What's the approximate attendance of your entire Sunday school program (Nursery through Adult)? ________

14. If you would like information on other *Custom Curriculum* courses, or other youth products from David C. Cook, please fill out the following:

Name: ____________________
Church Name: ____________________
Address: ____________________
____
Phone: (____) ____________________

Thank you!